Light Enters the Grove

Light Enters the Grove

Exploring Cuyahoga Valley National Park through Poetry

Edited by Charles Malone, Carrie George, and Jason Harris

The Kent State University Press ⬚ *Kent, Ohio*

ISBN 978-1-60635-485-8
Published in the United States of America

Cataloging information for this title is available at the Library of Congress.

28 27 26 25 24   5 4 3 2 1

CONTENTS

FOREWORD

Biodiversity in Cuyahoga Valley National Park

The poems in this collection introduce plants and animals that you might encounter in Cuyahoga Valley National Park. They tell us something about the life histories of different species and their strategies for survival. They also reflect how people value nature and learn lessons to better understand the human experience. While each poem reflects on an individual species, holistically I find that the poems provide a marvelous introduction to Cuyahoga Valley National Park's biodiversity.

What is biodiversity? Scientists use the term to describe the richness of life on earth. They measure biodiversity, in part, through an inventory of plants and animals found in a place. Cuyahoga Valley National Park's inventory shows a relatively high level of biodiversity for northeast Ohio. To date, 1,167 plants, 42 mammals, 20 reptiles, 22 amphibians, 65 fish, and 241 bird species have been recorded in the park. We expect this number to grow, especially as we learn more about less well-documented groups of animals such as insects.

Why does the park have higher biodiversity? The biggest drive is habitat diversity, which is influenced by the park's climate, soils, and topography. Geography also plays a role. The park sits on the Glaciated Allegheny Plateau, a region of flat uplands dissected by steep valleys. The plateau represents the western edge of the Appalachian Mountains before they give way to the Great Plains. While eastern species are more common in the park, western species may be found. Western species, such as coyote and some grassland birds, are also aided by land-use changes that have increased the open habitats that they prefer.

The park's location on migratory flyways also contributes to biodiversity. The valley provides a natural north-south corridor for birds and insects traveling between northern breeding grounds and southern wintering areas. Migration peaks in May when songbirds in their colorful breeding plumage—including 36 species of warblers—follow the river's path northward in great numbers. However, migrants add to biodiversity for much more of the year. Waterfowl migration, for example, peaks in March and November. Also adding to biodiversity is the valley's role as both a summer and winter destination, depending on species. For example, while the park is a summer breeding destination for wood ducks, buffleheads, a duck species that breeds in Canada and Alaska, may spend the winter here.

Monarch migration is a striking biodiversity story. The delicacy of the butterfly's fragile wings contrasts with the endurance of long-distance travel. Monarchs spend the winter in mountain forests of central Mexico. In early March, they leave the forests, mate, and seek the nearest milkweed fields in southern portions of the United States to lay their eggs. It takes three or four generations to migrate north. Each generation journeys progressively northward mating, laying eggs, and dying along the way. The summer monarchs that we see in Cuyahoga Valley are Generation 3. Some stay to breed, and others venture across Lake Erie into Canada. In the fall, we see Generation 4 heading south. These individuals will make it all the way to Mexico, overwinter there, and then start the cycle again.

In addition to location, the valley's habitat diversity is a major player in species diversity. The park's rugged terrain shaped by glaciers and eroding rivers underpins habitat diversity. The uplands, valley slopes, ravines, valley floor, and river all have different environmental conditions that support different habitats, thus different mixes of plants and animals. To illustrate biodiversity connected to habitat, consider the differences between bottomland and upland forests.

Bottomland forests flank the Cuyahoga River and its tributaries. These are moist areas that can experience periodic flooding. Sycamore trees, with distinctive white trunks, and quick-growing eastern cottonwoods dominate these forests. Other key trees include box elder maple and, in slightly higher areas, black cherry, buckeye, and slippery elm. Bottomland forests provide nesting places for a variety of birds. Screech owls make their homes in hollow trees, and Baltimore orioles build their hanging nests. Other nesting birds include yellow-throated warblers, cerulean warblers, American redstarts, orchard orioles, and blue-gray gnatcatchers. Opossum, fox, squirrel, coyote, and long-tailed weasel join the birds in using this habitat. Spring wildflowers can bloom profusely in moist ravines before the leaves of the canopy shade the forest floor. The visual treat includes bloodroot, Virginia bluebell, white trout lily, skunk cabbage, and squirrel corn.

In contrast, drier forests are found on the slopes and uplands of the Cuyahoga Valley. Common trees depend on the age of the forest. White, red, and black oaks and a variety of hickories, including shagbark and bitternut, beech, and sugar maples, are common in more mature forests. Younger forests—those farmed more recently—are often dominated by bigtooth aspen, white ash, and tulip poplar. Wildflowers, including rue anemone, wild geranium, and round-lobed hepatica, are most common in the spring before the leaf canopy blocks the light. Birds that find their nesting requirements met in upland forests include hooded warblers, ovenbirds, blue-headed vireos, scarlet tanagers, broad-wing hawks, and wood thrushes. Other upland forest animals include grey and southern flying squirrels, raccoons, red foxes, and coyotes.

Wetland habitats generally support the valley's greatest diversity. These are places where water is held on the landscape, shaping soils and vegetation. Many wetlands occur in low points, especially along the river. However, not all are in the valley's bottomlands. Clay soils can trap water on the valley walls, creating slope wetlands. Vernal pools form in upland depressions. These are temporary wetlands that fill during the spring rainy season and serve as breeding areas for many amphibian species.

In total, the park has more than 1,500 wetlands. Covering 70 acres, Beaver Marsh is among the largest. Because the Towpath Trail includes a boardwalk over Beaver Marsh, it is also among the most accessible. Beaver Marsh is a complex of wetland communities that are connected by water and influenced by beaver activity. The wetland hydrology changes from place to place within the marsh, and the plant composition changes with it. Groundwater feeds the marsh from both the north and south. Where this occurs, skunk cabbage is prevalent. Surface water runoff from Howe Meadow, which may have higher temperatures and nutrients, enters from the west and results in more pollution-tolerant vegetation near Riverview Road. Beaver dams create deepwater areas where only certain types of plants like fragrant water lily and spadderdock thrive.

Small changes in the landscape further contribute to biodiversity. Microclimates exist in cool, moist areas, such as around the Virginia Kendall Ledges. In these locations, relic populations from colder and wetter time periods survive. Eastern hemlock trees are common in those areas. Slumps, where a portion of the valley wall has slipped, host their own species compositions with unusual diversity. These are favorite places of botanists who look for unique plant species such as Indian paintbrush and whorled milkweed. When trees fall in the forest, they create sunny openings that become hot spots for plants that like to grow quickly.

Not all the park's biological diversity can be explained by natural conditions. Some results from the valley's human history. Prior to European settlement, forests and wetlands dominated Ohio and the Cuyahoga Valley. By the nineteenth century, most of the valley's forests had been replaced by farm fields. As agriculture gave way to outdoor recreation as the primary land use in the valley, farm fields began to convert back to forest. Meadows still grow in some of the more recently abandoned farm fields. As these meadows mature through the natural process of succession, they will develop into thickets and eventually back into forests. In many places, the National Park Service has hurried this process through tree planting. We have also undertaken major restoration projects where harsher land uses—mining, dumping, and development—followed agriculture as a land use.

The National Park Service has high value for biodiversity, but the sheer number of species isn't the final goal for parks. First and foremost, the National Park Service prioritizes protecting healthy natural ecosystems in which natural processes can occur unimpeded by people. Predator-prey relationships, safe passage of migratory species, and natural flow of water and nutrients are examples of valued natural processes. The editors organized the poems in this collection by habitat. This approach makes sense from a National Park Service perspective. National parks emphasize habitat protection as a primary means to protect species. The amount of biodiversity that results depends on the natural levels of biodiversity for the habitat. At Cuyahoga Valley, as natural conditions improve through natural succession and active restoration efforts, we will have more mature, less fragmented forests. Under those conditions, the number of species in the park inventory may drop.

One area where the National Park Service specifically works to protect biodiversity is in fulfilling our mandate to protect threatened and endangered species. Bats are of particular concern. The Indiana bat was listed as an endangered species in the 1960s and was last found in the valley in the early 2000s. In summer, they typically roost behind the exfoliating bark of large, often dead, trees. To protect Indiana bats, when projects require tree removal, we avoid doing so during roosting season.

Unfortunately, the situation for bats has worsened since the 1960s. More than half of the 47 bat species in the United States—including the Indiana bat—survive winter by hibernating in colonies. Hibernating bats are susceptible to a disease called white-nosed syndrome (WNS), caused by a fungus that grows on their muzzle, ears, and wings. Infected bats display abnormal behaviors, such as flying during daytime in winter. These behaviors cause bats to expend unnecessary energy and use up their winter fat reserves prematurely. Devastation from WNS has been severe. In some areas, 90 to 100 percent of bats have died. As a result, the northern long-eared bat is also now listed as an endangered species. To help slow the spread of WNS, the National Park Service had closed Ice Box Cave—a once-popular stop along the Ledges Trail—to public access. We have kept it closed to provide surviving bats a place to hibernate and roost without additional stress from human disturbance.

While biodiversity isn't the primary end goal for natural resource protection, the National Park Service recognizes that biodiversity is a cornerstone of healthy ecosystems. When individual species are missing, ecosystem health can drop. Imagine a river or stream without associated wetland plants to filter water, removing heavy metals and excessive levels of nutrients. Or imagine a forest without bacteria, fungi, and beetles to serve as decomposers that break down dead animal and plant material to release nutrients for the next generation of life.

Among the diverse species that play into ecosystem health, loss of pollinators poses among the greatest threats. Most pollinators are insects that spread pollen as they travel from flower to flower seeking nectar. In doing so, they fertilize the flowers, starting the creation of seeds and future young plants. Pollinator populations have dropped precipitously due to pesticides and other threats. Their loss threatens agriculture as well as natural systems. The National Park Service has planted native field flowers at trailheads and Boston Mill Visitor Center to bolster pollinator populations.

For park managers, biodiversity is also important as a primary window into evaluating the health of the natural environment and a means to monitor change. At Cuyahoga Valley National Park, we feel successful when we find sensitive species that indicate the improved health of the Cuyahoga River ecosystem. Examples include two-lined salamanders that require healthy headwater streams and darter fish that require healthy streams with clean water and riffles. Because we are seeing more sensitive species, we feel that the Cuyahoga River is ready to restore populations of another key group of animals—mussels that feed the food web in the river's sediments. Work on this effort has begun.

Monitoring biodiversity is helping to document the biggest disruptor to natural systems, climate change. The impacts of climate change are especially evident when looking at biodiversity on a larger geographic scale than a single park. Species distribution is shifting northward as climates warm. Prairie warblers have become more common in the valley, and changing climate is suspected be a driver. Climate change is also increasing the rate of spread of invasive species and pests. Park resource managers worry that we will lose eastern hemlocks in the park as their range shifts north. The introduction of pests due to human activities increases the threat. Hemlock woolly adelgid, a type of insect, is killing eastern hemlock trees farther east. It appeared in Shenandoah National Park in the late 1980s, and as many as 80 percent of the hemlocks there have died due to infestation. Keeping it from spreading here is a major challenge.

There is also the human value for biodiversity. One of these values is well reflected in this poetry collection—the value of biodiversity for inspiring awe, wonder, and a connection to place. The poems remind us that the variety of life on our planet is fascinating, and discovery is fun. I hope that reading it prompts you to consider and write about your own connections to nature. By creating these personal connections, we build a constituency for the protection of natural ecosystems. Biodiversity is a signature of national parks. They are places where protecting high-quality habitats is prioritized. As a result, they become a refuge for biodiversity on a larger scale. However, it takes a wider network of connected, protected spaces to ensure species survival. People caring about what happens in parks, their communities, and their yards is essential. Seeing and appreciating the world in new ways is a key step in that direction.

Jennie Vasarhelyi
Chief of Interpretation, Education, Visitor Services
Cuyahoga Valley National Park
July 2023

EDITORS' INTRODUCTION

Beginnings

To introduce this collection, we'd like to invite you on a walk. And on that journey, take a few pauses to note how each of us editors—Carrie George, Jason Harris, and Charlie Malone—came to the park differently. These differences play a key role in how we were able to gather this range of poems. This introduction braids our hike and personal stories together. Our walk will follow the organization of this collection and also one of Charlie's favorite hikes, a loop starting and ending at the Jaite Trailhead that threads its way through the diverse habitats that the park protects. Field to Forest to Water.

It was Carrie's involvement in poetry that pulled her into the park. She moved to northeastern Ohio for college. Yet, it was only during the pandemic as we launched this project that she started walking the trails and paying attention. Flashes of red-headed birds in the late-winter bare trees. Sharp greens peeking behind leaf litter. Angry geese. Chipmunks scuttling in the brush. Slowly, she learned the names of things. Two years later, she could differentiate dame's rocket from phlox, a downy woodpecker from a red-bellied. She could spot mayapple and jewelweed off the trail. When she explained this joy to her naturalist brother who helped her cultivate the curiosity she experienced outdoors, he said when you start to recognize the nonhuman beings around you, "it's like you're greeting a whole lot of friends." The park is where she regularly meets them.

Cuyahoga Valley National Park is the first park Jason ever cared about. This caring wouldn't start, though, until 2014. Growing up in a Black, working-class family in West Virginia, his traveling experiences were limited. For road trips and vacations, his family—and thus himself by hivemind—wished to leave the Appalachian lifestyle behind to revel in the noise of major cities that seemed to have more to offer than the quiet mountains and hillsides he was raised in. After moving to Cleveland, Ohio, in August 2014, he realized—then more than a hundred miles away from West Virginia and the nature and wildlife that sat just outside the doorstep of his childhood home—that he missed being surrounded by trees and wild animals and mountains and creeks. He missed what being around an ecosystem he was both a part of and apart from did for his emotional, physical, and psychological health. In an effort to assuage the absence he felt for nature, he searched "parks near me" and was directed—by Google—to the Ohio Towpath Trail. It was on the Towpath Trail where Jason started to feel a connection, a visceral and corporeal connection, to Cuyahoga Valley National Park.

Charlie first visited the park as a runner in high school, competing against Woodridge on a course that took on Kendall Hill. He rediscovered it as a camp counselor in college assisting a naturalist, Ron Etling, who knew the names, uses, and stories of every living thing in the park. He then began visiting as often as possible in each season before moving away from Ohio. The forests and sandstone formations reminded him of the woods behind the farm he grew up on in Geauga County. Moving back to Kent a few years ago, it was returning to CVNP, which really felt like home. The Wick Poetry Center, where he works, now brings sixty-plus campers to stay in the park as part of their summer camp each year.

In the simplest terms, for this project we invited writers with a connection to the park to explore and share their relationship with it. Each writer chose one species to celebrate—one mammal, one fungus, or one bird. A delight in the process of collecting poetry contributions was distributing species to writers. We amassed a spreadsheet of species found in Cuyahoga Valley National Park using iNaturalist and the recent BioBlitz data collected by community members. From that spreadsheet, Carrie used a random number generator to select three species for each writer to choose from. She received many responses expressing personal connections to species that had been randomly chosen for them. Writers responding, "I know that from my childhood," or, "I have a special nickname for that bird." Us walking a trail together, pointing our fingers to the ground, sky, saying, "Look! Do you see it too?"

This collection is an invitation to explore with each writer. Get your hands muddy in the eastern red-backed salamander's habitat. Crane your neck down to the twisted lung of the Jack-in-the-pulpit. Learn the names of sassafras and strangers. Wake to spring with trillium's tri-petaled bloom.

Field

We'll start our visit near Jaite. Jaite was the site of an old company town and paper mill. Now it houses the park headquarters and gives us access to the full range of ecosystems in the park. We head south, crossing the open floodplains west of the river to connect with the Buckeye Trail. Grassy fields surround the park's headquarters. Where the trail strays far enough from the Cuyahoga, meadows thrive. The line between grassland and wetland at the bottom of the valley is blurry. Our shoes get wet. Red-winged blackbirds call out while diving then swoop and cling to the tall grasses.

Jason fell first for Cuyahoga Valley National Park through sound, then sight. It began with the matter-of-fact call of red-winged blackbirds, both male and female. It took a minute, but eventually he discovered the source of the call perched high on a low tree sitting along the bank of the Cuyahoga River. Jason made figure eights on the path until he figured out which low tree the bird was calling from, then pulled his bicycle off to the side of the trail and looked up at a black bird with a flash of red shoulder patches. At the time, he didn't know the name of the bird, just that its call—which he learned later that day—was made year-round, in flight, while feeding, and to raise alarm when trouble rears its head.

After learning the call and plumage of the red-winged blackbird, Jason returned to it time and time again, as if it were his home. For him, visiting the valley—and in some way living with these certain birds within this ecosystem—was not enough. Eventually, he purchased a set of binoculars and traveled around different parts of the Cuyahoga Valley to see them up close. When birdwatching reached its peak for him, Jason then went out and purchased a voice recorder for the sole purpose of recording soundscapes set against the distinct red-winged blackbird's trill. After a while, he not only wanted to see them up close, but he did. Jason wanted to carry their alarm in his pocket, into his home, and he found a way to.

It is in these same fields that Delilah McCrea finds milkweed and this powerful metaphor:

I'm trying to find
a way through death
like the monarch butterflies
who feed on milkweed toxins
to make themselves
distasteful to predators.

These poems sometimes face the facts of the natural world and find vital metaphors like this, and other times find mirrors for our very human concerns in the species. The fields themselves are both metaphor and fact, both the imprint of human activity and the reclamation of some kind of wilderness. Throughout the park, anywhere humans cleared the trees, for farming or the Richfield Coliseum, grassland and prairie ecosystems have filled that vacancy. There are more grasses than any of us can identify: switchgrass, poverty grass, bromegrass, timothy, and rye—more than 90 species of grass and 70 species of sedges.

And among the swaying stalks, what else? A monarch butterfly or eastern tiger swallowtail flitting from milkweed bushels. Killdeer, American robins, and song sparrows calling to their kin. Maybe the white pom-pom of the eastern cottontail flicks the patch of queen anne's lace as it flees. Somewhere across the way, a coyote waits. Somewhere above, a turkey vulture circles.

Forest

We cross Riverview Road looking for the Buckeye Trail to carry us north toward Station Road Bridge. After traversing a wetland on a boardwalk, the trail follows a lush but modest creek whose name, if it exists, we don't know. Yet all along its banks are species that have been in our heads for months.

Climbing up to the west rim of the valley then back down along the canalway, we'll see more plants and animals that are present in this collection. It's early spring; we see bullfrogs and spring peepers, and painted turtles are sunning themselves on logs. The sugar maples are waking. Bloodroot runs riot on the damp hills. Some of these will fade; others will thrive. The mayapples are just getting started. In a week, trillium will start to grow. Poison ivy and its remedy, jewelweed, will arrive in summer. The cicadas will sing about it. And Cathy Barber writes about this song in her beautiful golden shovel poem for the cicada:

> Presently,
> we walk again, mount the steps to the house. It
> suddenly feels a big world and we small creatures in it, hoping we will
> make our own tremendous noise before we die.

What we bring back to our homes, our lives from our time in the park is invaluable. It is the reason we offer it our attention and why we return seeking new trails and new sounds.

Rivers, Lakes, Ponds, and Wetlands

After a few hours walking beneath the trees, we follow Chippewa Creek to Station Road Bridge at Pinery Narrows and cross the Cuyahoga on an old steel bridge made by the Massillon Bridge Company. Following the

towpath south along the river, one sees many species that we wish some-
one had responded to. How did no one choose the yellow trout lily? Our
first snake arrived late in this collection, and three garters slip off into the
dry leaves. Is the poet's narcissus even native? How did we all resist its
temptation?! We're getting worked up again. And that's the point. There
is so much available to us in the park. And each time we come, the sea-
sons have ticked forward just a little and everything changes.

The poems of the wetlands celebrate the strange star jellies and elusive
otters. Geoffrey Polk's poem for the water lily describes these changes
perfectly:

> Out of the muck of Northeast Ohio
>   out of the Cuyahoga valley
> out of this mud-clotted shallow pond
>   bordered by towpath and scenic railroad
> jogged past by runners, bicycle sprinters,
>   strollers and Sunday photographers,
> interrupted periodically by sound blasts
>   to scare crows from corn fields,
> they appeared one day on the pond's surface,

If we are lucky enough to cross Beaver Marsh between the Ira Trailhead
and Hunt's Farm the day those spectacular lotuses open, it's hard not to
be moved. Many of the poems in this collection are playful, especially
those in the wet with swamp water. Take Bob King's poem for the red-
headed ground beetle or Catherine Wing speaking through the voice of
the muskrat:

> My family's ancient and well-represented
> in the fossil record. I am rumored to be descended from the Balkan Snow
> Vole with whom I share a molar.
> I can swim backwards and I can hold my breath
> for a full 17 minutes. Are you good for that?

We love when these poets play, when they tell the story or share the science of these species, when they flip our preconceptions, when they reject our human ideas, and when they build a nest out of them.

Conclusion and Gratitude

Each contribution represents an act of care. Whether recounting a memory with a specific species, as in Hilary Plum's "Painted-Cup Paintbrush" or Jeff Gundy's "Musclewood"; lamenting loss, as in Dan Dorman's "A Great Blue Heron"; expressing guilt, as in Benjamin Rhodes's "White-Tailed Deer"; or offering praise, as in Bronlynn Thurman's "Resounding through the Brush & Branch" and Kari Gunter-Seymour's "A Windfall of American Robins"; the pieces within this collection recognize the species of our National Park as complete, lively, and unique organisms that deserve witness, compassion, and dignity. Erin Sharkey writes in her contribution to *A Darker Wilderness: Black Nature Writing from Soil to Stars,* "Nature is a relationship, a big map of interconnectedness, of needs met, bodies transformed." Each piece in *Light Enters the Grove: Exploring Cuyahoga Valley National Park through Poetry* places a marker on our "big map of interconnectedness," allowing us to explore deeper, farther off trail, and submit to the transformation that follows.

Amid the worsening climate crisis, this collection offers an approach to deepening urgency and action in reacting to our planet's transformation: We must not be strangers to our ecosystems. If we are most likely to extend care to those closest to us, we must invite nature closer.

These poems, like the park, live at the intersection between our personal experiences, our public and political actions, and the needs of a healthy ecosystem. These spheres bleed into one another. Our work was to invite different perspectives. To let the ecotone, or transitions between biological communities, be complicated.

Carrie came to the park as a solitary experience but grew into its folds through time spent with others. Leading fourth graders on hike and write field trips along the Station Road Bridge Trailhead, she peered through time at what once was her, bending down to pick up an especially vibrant leaf or arching her small neck to a treetop searching for a screech owl in a distant cavity. She listened to these students wonder how long a human-made bridge would last and gawk at the once-mighty canal, now a skeleton under an eagle's nest. When once a wooly bear caterpillar passed along the trail ahead of them, a group of boys crouched to help it cross. "See," they said, "boys can be gentle too." Like any good fairy tale, we leave the woods different than when we enter. Reading the poems in this collection has invited a similar transformation. Each contributor announcing how they, too, have learned their own gentleness or ferocity or even love.

For Jason, his earliest experiences with Cuyahoga Valley National Park made him a smarter, more observant person and a keen listener not only to the call of red-winged blackbirds but many other birds as well. Writing this introduction felt like what it felt like to be Black, an Appalachian, and a writer documenting his life amid the Anthropocene. It was difficult. Difficult not because he didn't have the right words to say, but difficult because there were too many words to say. What could he say about Cuyahoga Valley National Park that hasn't already been said—on a state and a national level? His hope, for anyone who reads this collection of poems, is that you are—as he has been—guided to see the beauty around you, even if it begins in a state of not knowing the call we hear often but don't yet know the name of.

Charlie had the joy of encouraging writers in Colorado to take on a similar project with Rocky Mountain National Park, the only park he has ever come close to knowing as well as he knows Cuyahoga Valley. Ever since, he has wanted to bring this project home. He was so curious to see what perspectives this invitation would bring in, so eager to be surprised—he has not been disappointed. For this project to be successful, the invitation has to continue; it has to encourage each reader to return and to take an interest in the health of our park.

When Wick Poetry Center teaching artists work with young people at our overnight writing camp in CVNP, we emphasize the fact that US

National Parks belong to all of us. They are federal lands cultivated and protected for the preservation of natural wonders, open to public access. Still, people of color and lower-income Americans are far less likely to visit National Parks than white, wealthy, and middle-class Americans. It is also critical to remember that this valley has been lived in for more than 14,000 years. One of our goals in curating this collection was to widen the expanse of nature writing to include those traditionally excluded from the genre. We also encouraged contributors to push the boundaries of traditional nature writing by experimenting with form, archive, and content. In order to document the contemporary relationship between the human and nonhuman world—complete with anxiety, hope, reverence, distance, and inexplicable closeness—the traditions of nature writing must adapt, as living things so often do.

We hope this collection follows in the footsteps of similar projects, like *A Poetic Inventory of Rocky Mountain National Park; Cascadia Field Guide: Art, Ecology, Poetry; The Sonoran Desert: A Literary Field Guide;* and the place-based anthologies that are sprouting elsewhere. We hope it will continue to raise awareness about the resources and work of National Parks, as well as continue conversations of access in nature writing, outdoor spaces, and professional fields relating to the environment.

We are grateful to all the contributors of *Light Enters the Grove: Exploring Cuyahoga Valley National Park through Poetry.* We were lucky to complete this project with an abundance of pieces from local writers, many of whom could not fit in the bounds of this print edition. We invite you to view the full collection as well as an interactive map of the park at cvnp.travelingstanzas.com/poetic-inventory.

So many folks have helped this project along; thank you all. Particular gratitude is due to Hailey Rinier, Olivia Farina, the team at Each + Every for their illustrations, and everyone at the Kent State University Press.

I Field

Coyote, *Canis latrans*

COYOTE IN THE VALLEY

Stephanie Ginese

In the hushed plum of twilight
      I hear You

wild chanteuse
      charming the dark
            behind teeth made of moon

stay hidden, shadow shifter
      for the dog of us understands you
      not

the pitch of your feral song carries

                  sacred story after sacred story

You laughed & the world was   You laugh & the world is

resilient wilderness
in honest pursuit of somewhere we are not.

PAINTED-CUP PAINTBRUSH

Hilary Plum

problem of naming starts young
in the woods
pond the size of a lake and manmade
dammed up and smoothly
rising industrial banks   shitty little playground
to the sound of the dog-pound's dogs barking and
goose shit
everywhere   plastic buoys marked the safe
or allowed space, my brother a lifeguard
the camp counselors all tried to flirt with but
he scanned and scanned the water
for disappearing children
                        contrary to popular
drowning is silent and subtle, lack of wave
lack of splash
                        contrary to
it was then called, the flower, "Indian Paintbrush"
I looked for it red orange yellow in the low
surprise of the woods, endlessly fine up close or a smear
of bright color in Connecticut   the problem
with the name not something a child could finally name
or not me   the place is inscribed and you are
with a long violence whose paths are your own, around
the pond with bright paint on bark marking and your white
ancestors insisting in Latin "he who is transplanted"
                        "Bicentennial Pond"
I circled and circled it to grow up
nothing   could be more perfect than finding
silent and bright that flower the paintbrush

somewhere beyond and amid
geese honking raucous, Canadian bird-clowns
shit slick beneath kid feet   "still sustains"
we moved away
taking books, dishes, leaving my orange room
within the paintbrush's big exquisite territory
        "endangered in Connecticut"

Painted-Cup Paintbrush, *Castilleja coccinea*

Killdeer, *Charadrius vociferus*

EVERYONE KNOWS A KILLDEER MEANS NO HARM

Mary Biddinger

Find me by the ditch.
Least glamorous stretch
of dreadful meadow,
former scrap heap turned
cold cruising spot.
You wouldn't let kids
sleep here. How
could anything
rest in this gravel-scape:
runaway trash corner,
riverbank of zero
picnic tables, no
hammocks or guitars?
Enjoy my broken-wing
act, legs like stems.
Body loose newspaper.
Song, or scream?
If we both believe
I'm hurt and dangerous,
maybe it's true.

Eastern Cottontail, *Sylvilagus floridanus*

RUNNING

Eros Livieratos

I found you—running
escaping the noise
of everything. Grazing
in man-made suburbs. You
harbor no malice.

Easily fraught, plush, and
small—
a man once told me,
you are "barely worth
the kill. Too thin. Gamey."

He does not know
the community you make
the joy you bring
when I park my car and find
you scurrying somewhere else.

In the rain, you cover
under branches and bushes.
In warmth, you love
openly. Reproduce,
nested in the ground.

As seasons change,
I will look out
for more of you
nesting, running—
living in the twilight.

Eastern Tiger Swallowtail, *Papilio glaucus*

PAPILIO GLAUCUS

Kira Preneta

when we met
on a shaded bridge

facing the Sweet Water Sea

I couldn't fathom
3 broods &

every year taking in
enough green to

spin   out
on a limb

imagining
a light

blue on yellow
on green

another generation
waking in fields of blades

the park freshly mown

American Robin, *Turdus migratorius*

A WINDFALL OF AMERICAN ROBINS

Kari Gunter-Seymour

flit-flap the valley on this balmy,
budding dawn, festoon
unwitting branches in glints red-orange.
Dozens splash in the creek,
sing with rusted tongues—
the language of risen grass,
tepid rain, laughing toddlers.

Sky a mass of mists, sunbeams
blink ochre and auburn
across dew-gilded meadows,
the light an illusion of wonder
and awe, as if the scrim
between life and death has thinned,
is penetrable, if only we trill tenderly,
fling open windows and doors,
until the house becomes air.

Pearl Crescent, *Phyciodes tharos*

CUYAHOGA VALLEY'S DISSENT COLLAR 2020

Monica Kaiser

In Memoriam Ruth Bader Ginsburg

I am cocooning,
& visualizing butterflies
to escape the dying,

the images
of people with tubes
down their throats.

A global diseasing.

Mother keeps warning.
Mother keeps warming.

I am guilty of climate genocide,
even as I fell in love
        with you, pearl crescent.
Even as I watched
        natural laws govern you,
summer after summer,
the continual reinvention
of yourself—
a finale of flames
        puddled on wet ground,
an otherworldly orange.

Language-like,
your pigments & patterns

are fluid, vary state to state,
        region to region. Your pearls
are persistent, rebellious by nature.

One by one,
you flitter, disperse.
        Heavenwards,
out of sight. Down to open
meadows, to the throats & tubes
of flowers. Petal posers.
        Wings open. Wings close.

Your proboscis sips the nectar's sweetness,
as tiny spiracles allow air
        into your tracheal tubes.

Systems are necessary for survival—
        as is your courtship chase,
a possible fluttering, a coupling,
a joining of abdomens: copulation.

I, too, am a reinvention—
a dynamic energy
sheltering inside a bulldozed tree
as it snows,
as our gas furnace heats,
as our curtains shiver in its air,
as I visualize butterflies

& reimagine you & your
hindwing's crescent pearls
quivering at the collar
of every
star.

WOOLLY BEAR: AUTUMNAL PARADE

Leah Graham

time glides by
on skinned knees

a monarch drinks
the last drops of sunlight

chlorophyll crumbles
in symphonic prisms

inflated tires crunch
across crushed limestone

the caravan commences
a big top circus production

strider and single speeds
trailer and orange erect flag waving

goldenrods
fade brown

yellow leaves burst
overstory

thoughts patter
along a warm breeze

circling
a reflection of sky

feet pedal
swerve near the Cuyahoga

training wheels rattle and clank
Mama, I love you

squeals of joy
bells *thrring*

a dry leafy spot
red flushed cheeks and salty hair

singing echoes reverberate
under corrugated steel tunnel

hidden overpass
watchful eyes

plop of frog in
murky canal

soft call of geese
sunbathing sliders

preening mallard
stalking heron

honeybees calculate
on clover

we follow
undulating woolly bears

soaking in
this autumnal equinox

Isabella's tiger moth
take refuge

we cycle

Isabella Tiger Moth, *Pyrrharctia isabella*

PENINS

OH

32'30"   455

850

BR 696

Boston

750

800

nsula

BM
817

750

Haskell

CORP.

Ritchie

CORP

Run

881

Golf Course

Poison Hemlock, *Conium maculatum*

POISON HEMLOCK
Jonathan Conley

w—
       hat
can poise
on a poison
       he—
mlock
hard
       hard hair
or
the attn: I deserve
       to b—

e poised
       poisoned
upon
an eye
       & eye well

Turkey Vulture, *Cathartes aura*

THE TURKEY VULTURE
Andrew Gilkey

Wings coast to coast,
a black scar on
the belly of the sky.
A red ruddy head scanning
roadside carrion.
I, an ecological equalizer.
An envoy of all forgotten gods of death.
The bluebird's foil.
A feather for every gust guiding
thermal air that pushes me upwards, pushes
the smell of rot into my septumless nose.
My baldness isn't pattern,
It's by design,
It's a clean glove gripping a scalpel's handle
picking meat from vacated
vessels to plunge bacteria bound flesh
into corrosive guts.
The sound of bone-scraping
is the lounge jazz of our night-time committees.
intermingling with our prehistoric chatter
as we look up to morning stars,
dreaming of the next day's reaping.

I PLANT MILKWEED ON MY FATHER'S GRAVE

Delilah McCrea

because the plant is so named
for the sticky white latex that
pours out of wounded tissues

and my father like
his father before him
died from cellular wounds
he received after a lifetime
in rubber factories.

I'm trying to find
a way through death
like the monarch butterflies
who feed on milkweed toxins
to make themselves
distasteful to predators.

Or maybe
I'm stumbling past death
like my step father,
who's managed to out live my mother
despite feeding on the toxins of
the Hospira Pharmaceutical plant by day
and thirty packs of Busch Light by night.

I promise
when I swallow the milkweed

from your grave.
I'm not thinking of the latex,
or your cancer.
I'm thinking of the genus
Asclepias so named for
the Greek god of medicine.

I want to be healed.
I swear it.

Common Milkweed, *Asclepias syriaca*

Poverty Oat grass, *Danthonia spicata*

POVERTY OAT GRASS / SUBSISTENCE
Haylee Schwenk

This plant can grow anywhere—sun, shade,
sand, shallow topsoil, no water for weeks. It's like
living on government cheese, powdered milk,
mcintosh apples that ended up in golden delicious bags,
chicken necks making the broth for soup.

This plant is putting out flowers half the summer,
waiting for cross-fertilization, but just in case
it turns out to be a bad year here's a self-
pollinating bud in reserve. It's like hoping that man
will keep a job, putting the baby in a dresser drawer to sleep,
handing down the shoes through all six kids.

This plant twirls curly dry leaves around its base—
protective, decorative, maybe a fire hazard—
making a party out of death. It's like scrounging enough sugar
for a raisin pie, borrowing a suit for the funeral,
splitting a beer after dinner when the kids have gone to bed.

SONG SPARROW
Virginia Konchan

Female song sparrows are smart and strategic:
they're attracted to not just the male's song,
but how well it reflects their ability to learn.
The greater the repertoire, and incorporation
of a song tutor's legacy, the better chances
the male has of capturing a female's heart.
Is the inversion of anthropomorphism our
understanding that birds are more evolved
than anthropoid's awkward mating dance?
Favoring brushland and marshes, sparrows
can also thrive in human-dominated areas:
suburbs, agricultural fields, and roadsides.
Their muted coloration of russet and gray
belie their unique gift of musical repartee:
onc of their songs resembles the opening
notes of Beethoven's Symphony No. 5.
A particular song is determined by pitch,
rhythm, and timbre, and most sparrows
know up to 1000 variations on 20 tunes.
Are not two sparrows sold for a penny?
Jesus asked his disciples, rhetorically.
And not one of them will fall to the
ground apart from your Father,
He said, in a parable about care.
Even the sparrow finds a home
where she may lay her young
at your altars, O Lord of hosts,
sang King David in the Psalms.
Sparrows distinguish between

neighbors and strangers among
them on the basis of their songs,
and shuffle and repeat their songs
as if curating a Spotify playlist.
To hear them is to feel alive;
to be thought of as a symbol
of God's concern for creation
is no less astounding, it's true.
Creator of muses, music, flight:
I'm trilling these songs for you.

Song Sparrow, *Melospiza melodia*

Common Dandelion, *Taraxacum officinale*

NOTHING COMMON ABOUT THIS DANDELION

Cora McCann Liderbach

With yellow petals spiky as lions' teeth • the dandelion surveys
its grass terrain • unbowed by a reputation • for heedless
propagation • proud of the label *Taraxacum officinale* • less fond
of *cankerwort, wild endive, yellow gowan and puffball* •
but grateful for kids' pursed lips • to speed seeds along
with wishes • waft offspring for miles on pappus parachutes •
sending taproots deep into earth • aerating soil, dispersing nutrients •
stems stretching skyward • flowers reflecting sun, moon and stars •
celestial blessings • for a careless world

Monarch Butterfly, *Danaus plexippus*

MONARCH

Deborah Fleming

Transparent light of afternoon,
late summer chirr of cicadas
and the green frog's G-string note.

Ironweed blooms royal purple
like a glass of wine held up in air.

A monarch plucks sweetness
from the petals, carefully opening and closing
the stained glass of its translucent wings.

Wild Carrot, *Daucus carota*

D. CAROTA

Jessica Jones

Queen Anne's Lace—how many
at five in the evening
in August?
Can't count those in arms reach
—white, cream, green, gold,
mauve, white again;
snowflakes beaming face up,
some curled,
tentative

like girls at *Quinceañera.*

Others spread like matrons' aprons
wise in the truth of their short hour,
dispensing perfect acceptance
of time.
Instructing me
against bitter patience,
to embrace
their widening view—
tactful, elegant—

amid sifting light.

II Forest

Trillium, *Trillium grandiflorum*

TRILLIUM

Kimberlee Medicine Horn

I meander through the woods
looking for my springtime
absently loosed from my grasp
on the way into the
Autumn of my years.

I forget the value of
hunkering down into
the protective layers
of the earth in deep sleep.

In spring, my feet sink
slightly into the soil
off the path near
the trunk of the tree.

Under a collection of
brown and withered leaves,
the *trillium grandiflorum*
awaken.

I smooth the woodland cover
with deep joy in knowing
the next time I venture
into the woods, they'll be transcending
faith, hope, and love
in dewy white.

Interrupted Fern, *Osmunda Claytoniana*

THE INTERRUPTED FERN

Kathleen Cerveny

takes a moment for itself,
stopping briefly in its slow
unfolding from the forest floor
to spore itself for the future.
Within its tall and barren
vase of feathers the fertile
central fronds will pause
in the rote release of pinnae.

They take a breath—make space
along their spines to bloom
a nursery before resuming
the unfurling of their lissome blades.
With millennia of practice—
as far back as the Triassic—
these *Osmunda* have prevailed,
independent of an "other" for fulfillment.

Through eras of their seasonal decay,
these fragile ferns—which once sustained
Cretaceous herbivores—are layered, deep;
compressed into the midnight seams
now plundered by a fevered world.

White-Tailed Deer, *Odocoileus virginianus*

WHITE-TAILED DEER

Benjamin Rhodes

I'm sorry to say
the way I know you
best is strung-up
by your hind legs,
the cavity of your body
on display, headless,
skin flayed and peeled
to be cured and stretched
over a wooden stool later.

I'm sorry, your meat
was delicious as a pot
roast, your youth and lack
of fear at death made
the gravy, the potatoes
tender. If you didn't know
better, you might not tell
the flesh in your teeth
was once wild.

And no, I was never the one
with the bow, with the camouflaged
rifle and orange vest. I only ever
perched in boxes nailed to trees
as adventure in imagination, as
play at being higher than my
surroundings. I only ever saw
the way men in my family
treated you through pictures,
only ever pet your neck
as it hung on the wall.

American Sweetgum, *Liquidambar styraciflua*

AMERICAN SWEETGUM
Caryl Pagel

Work in the woods you're not an arborist

Go to the lake it's a flavor spike

Star-thorn seed-spurt gum-spike spike

Clouds go to pieces

One too many gusts you guess

Chipmunk warns by ding-dinging a tin hood

We won't get everything

*

It's a hard job if a woman wants it

Sharper than they'll ever be

How many leaves make a grievance tree

"It's happening everywhere"

The one in charge of listening turns

Otherwise it's easy

Almost anyone could

*

Kicking pods as if they're bark

All one can be is a wall at first

Keep the sap out

Count to four as you hum along

All the live-long live-long

Round and round the block again

Holding hands

Sassafras, *Sassafras albidum*

UNDERSTORIES
Andrea Imdacha

April morning laden with mother-child breath, unearthing treasures
from the underbelly of leaves. The sensation of being near-five, a
whole hand of years closing like my fist around Mother's calloused
fingertip, tugging her down the stooped back of a hill toward the
silver rush of water called River shushing over the shale where
Mother also whispers hush hush at my ululations.

My yellow rainboots, my yellow coat. Mother and I waddle, bills
to the ground, pecking out treasures. In her old pail, our trinkets
rattle. Mommy who is brimful of Names—

Sandstone, Silt, Bivalve.
                    Black Gum, Pawpaw, Redbud.
                                        Fern, Lichen, Hemlock.

I toe up fossils from the riverbed where sandbank skims forest.
Sloughed-off cauls of snow encircle the longtrees, nursing the
undergrowth that buds in treeshadow. A revelation of shoots sprout
skyward from the litterfall—green leaves egground or mitten-
gloved or cleaved into thirds, little ghosts with open arms,
beckoning.

"Sassafras," Mother singsongs, uprooting a sapling. Naming the
plant, Naming the child.

Mitten Tree in my toddling hands. Like Mother I chew the crisp
stems. Softmint from the soil where my foremothers are planted
awakens tender buds of taste. Invocation of pocketbook spearmint,
leather-perfumed, idling unwrapped in the undernook of Mother's

bag, reducing to chalk when toothed-apart in the grocery line. This taste blooms too, budding and becoming, a changeling on my tongue. Spring tonic. Rootbeer nights. Toothpaste dollops. Suggestion of soap awakening my tongue to bitterness. A revelation, too, when Mother overturns the leaves to expose ghostwhite underbellies inviting us to netherworlds.

Mint of the Woods. American Cinnamon. American Licorice so unlike anise from Fathersoil, where brownstars speckle Sri Lankan spice gardens and maybe, like sassafras, sprout in the understory, seeding the soil where my ancestors planted roots. Fatherland, that foreign place.

Freshgreen. Springpill.
                    Underwhite. Bittermint.

Such things I could say of myself, my whiteness under a surface
    browned by the sun. Bitter pills chewed like old purse-gum, disintegrating into the taste of my mouth so that my own saliva surfaces the memory of the words I swallowed, the kind that linger in the throat of a biracial girl whose childhood sprawls like sassafras down the Eastern coast.
                    Ohio outskirts,
                Carolina outskirts,
            Georgia outskirts atop red clay.
                                "Bloodsoil," new friends say, giving Name to what lies underfoot. Speaking of the abducted, the enslaved, the overtrodden, the emancipated, the reconstructed,

the segregated, the integrated, the profiled, the soilbound

Ancestors these new friends search for in the pruning scars of family trees. In recipes for gumbo thickened with sassafras like Father's recipe for crab curry over idiyappam—never written down, the memory buried alongside the spoon I used to steal tastes of Father-Mother-Sister-Brotherland—the lost continent, the lost island, the lost forests verdant with jungleleaf and riversand and treeshadow and waterrush and all the tastes the English stole, the Dutch stole, the Portuguese stole, the French stole, the Germans stole, the Belgians stole, the Spanish stole—and isn't your mouth tired, by now, of Naming multitudes made Thieves by

spicelust
 ricelust
  goldlust   indigolust
   tobaccolust
             cottonlust

                    sassafraslust

because remember sassafras moved across oceans too. Unsinkable sassafras hammered into the hulls of ships. Unbreachable sassafras fencing coops and crops and farms and villages and the bloodwet land and the Names we lifted—Erie, Yemassee, Yamacraw—for lakes and townships and bluffs severed from the sea.

Haint-leafed sassafras haunting the spring forests. Spirit Protector. Body Nourisher. Cleanser of bad blood. Purifier of souls.

"You can only do so much," I say to my son, nearly-five fingers of his life wrapping around me, returning life's balance to mother-child. Returning my feet to Ohio soil where Father rests, body-to-bone, deep beneath the mud browning our yellow boots.

"Sassafras," Mother says and my son reaches through the April fog to touch the sapling nestled in tombstone shade, the air still, warmwet, unseasonable. Almost a Georgia spring. I pluck three ghostleaves and we chew the stems to pulp, Naming all along.

Jewelweed, *Impatiens capensis*

BENEATH THE BLOOM

Judith Mansour

Jewelweed
Oxymoron of sorts
Kind of like, you're pretty
For a foreign girl, they said
When you're not even foreign
Or maybe you are but what does that matter
The thing with weeds is that they are not foreign
Indigenous
They just crop up
Like the convenience store your dad never had
Was accused of owning
'Cause he drove a Cadillac
Had olive skin
The thing with weeds is that
They're healers, sometimes
Hidden kindness
Jewelweed soothes
The relentless itch of poison ivy
Scratched so much that the skin breaks open
Starts to bleed
Generous in sap, zaps the pain
Like a hug from your mom when
Your third grade teacher called you a dirty Syrian
But you weren't dirty or Syrian
The parks and the woods
Where you're encouraged to hike
The scenic trails
Pretty with plants and vines and brush
That you cannot pick or pluck or take

For fear of fines, steep and harsh
The cost of living without knowing the rules
Refined flora, not mixed, cross pollinated
But all you saw was a tangle of green
With magnificent petals, buzzing with bees
Jewelweed is fine to satisfy an itch
After slumming in the woods
A shoulder to cry on, as it were
But you're not to be kept, brought home
In a crystal vase, a bouquet, God forbid
With that luscious bloom
That makes boys chase girls they won't love for real
Impatiens capensis
Irresistible nectar
Hummingbirds, butterflies
Lured, seduced by their exotic flesh
But we know better
The Spotted Touch-Me-Not
Is a weed
Invasive, intrusive
Assuming too much

MAY WE BE MORE HONEST
ABOUT WHAT WE ARE

KJ Cerankowski

*[The bald-faced hornet is not actually a hornet.
It is a yellowjacket wasp that, unlike its tawny cousins,
lacks yellow pigmentation. It is instead dressed in white
stripes and splotches—piebald, bald-faced,
as in a ghostly (ghastly?) white visage.]*

We call them so many things they are not: *hornet,*
     aggressive,
          bull wasp as if brutish
as if their sting is a random offensive, an attack
for lack of anything better or a lashing
     out with undue cause,
          unwarranted and reckless

I know too well how easily a defensive needle is mistaken
for aggression. I have been taken for the same—
vengeful, unable
     to let it go or forgive
          without calamity

Scientists believe wasps can remember faces in their particularity
each curve,
     crevice,
          angle of jaw and squint of eye—
this wasp will single out an invader whose face cannot
     be forgotten
          attacking only the one in a crowd

Perhaps there is a lesson here in letting go . . .

But who else will save us when we might have
      died but didn't?
Who else will counter the invasion,
      take the sting out
           of the wound?

In the face of the ghost: threat, a bite to ease
      the pain
           of another pain—

When they call you a monster, do not forget
every smile is full of teeth

Bald-Faced Hornet, *Dolichovespula maculata*

American Witch Hazel, *Hamamelis virginiana*

WINTER BLOOM
Quartez Harris

where seasons
      pass under new turquoise skies,
      where colors fall quietly in the forest
            where cold ponds flow under small wooden bridges,
            where snow
      crystals float along brisk tree bark, where leaves,
tangled twigs lay on the powdery, white ground
      there are flowers winter can't wilt
see the gnarl stem joyously budding a spidery yellow foliage
      in this thicket coldness, mottled gray moths flower
            in the wintry fog, settling on witch hazels.
      they disappear like the last colored leaf,
      leaving behind grains of seedling dust
from its scale glittered wings
      here the feral earth doesn't turn,
it sits.

WHITEHALL TERRACE

Sylvia Clark

Every year,
carpenter bees return
to their woodwork,
expanding the cracks
in the carport rafters,
like ice
to a stone,
like the pitted, filled cavities
of the rough quilt cement entrance.

But do the bees know wood
from what we rely on?

Do they not have their own constructions?

Do they know beam
from crucifix,
tree
from church?

Any good carpenter does.

But do they?

Every carpenter bee is holy,
as holy as honey,
as holy as the lion's skull,
the carports like the emaciated remains
of a beast.

In this Rust Belt town,
carpenter bees are oxygen.

Truly,
within every pollination
lies the power
for inspiration,
and
with decay
in every baby's breath,
we carve
into what was never ours
to begin
with,
what we call home.

Eastern Carpenter Bee, *Xylocopa virginica*

Eastern Tent Caterpillar Moth, *Malacosoma americana*

HOMEOWNERSHIP

Zachary Thomas

The third coat of *Eastern Tent Moth Wing* dried
as sundown beamed bright bronze boxes
onto the far living room wall
where wooden framed photographs of family, friends,
and purchased proof of this married project, this fixer upper,
    this welcome home
in need of TLC will rest above the hearth's flickered free
    flames forever
warmed by a single union, 1 life in Christ's name, we pray
for cracked cocoons and velvet flight paths to abandoned
    forests of
good health, loud laughs, and fancy fulfilling feasts right and
    just
for my floral crowned queen, beckoning me to join her
for our first supper together under this roof.

Pharaoh Cicada, *Magicicada septendecim*

CICADAS

Cathy Barber

a golden shovel after Matsuo Bashō
as translated by William George Aston

Back from a night out, on the
walk from garage to house, we're surrounded by the cry
of insects punching above their weight, of
tiny bodies expanding and contracting, the
unmistakable sound of cicada after cicada
out-louding each other. It gives
us pause, that total permeation, and we make no
movement for a minute, just listen as they sign-
al on the air, "I am here," hope that
a mate answers their call and life goes on. Presently,
we walk again, mount the steps to the house. It
suddenly feels a big world and we small creatures in it, hoping we will
make our own tremendous noise before we die.

MUSCLEWOOD

Jeff Gundy

for Nelson Strong

Blue Hen to Buttermilk Falls is an easy 20 minutes, even with the roots
and creek to slow you down. But it always took an hour with Nelson
who never saw a tree he couldn't explain, a patch of woods that didn't signify.

The Horne-bound tree is a tough kind of Wood, that requires so
much paines in riving as is almost incredible, being the best to
make bolles and dishes, not subject to cracke or leake.
   —William Wood, *New England's Prospect,* 1634

My farm boy half, always bent on arriving, sighed when Nelson stopped
at a gnarly little tree, its trunk no bigger than my calf, and said, *Oh,*
this is musclewood. The settlers tried to use it, he said, but found the wood
so tough they mostly gave up, learned to just let it be.

American Hornbeam. Leaves emerge reddish-purple, change to
dark green, go yellow to orange-red in fall. Blue-gray bar, fluted
with long, sinewy ridges. Difficult to transplant due to deep
spreading lateral roots. Slow growing. The hard wood is used to
make golf clubs, tool handles, and mallets.
   —The Morton Arboretum

Touch it, he said, and I wrapped a hand around the trunk,
a comfortable fit. My flesh still remembers the grooved bark,

how it spiraled upward like a long loose-threaded screw.
My hand told me the wood I clutched was dense, pale, stiff
beyond even the oaks and maples, ready to last a long time
between the trail and the creek, easy with a flood now and then.

The Ojibwe people used musclewood as ridgepoles in wigwams.
Decoctions of its bark were used in Cherokee, Iroquois, and
Delaware medicine to treat painful urination, "diseases peculiar
to women," and diarrhea, respectively.
  —The Heartwood Tree Company

Nelson moved west. I'm stuck at home. This absurd,
apocalyptic year creeps slowly toward God knows what.
But the little musclewood is still there, leaning into darkness
and day between the creek and trail, whirling and steady,
pressing out and shedding its new leaves and seeds and flowers,
tough as any tree or trail or creek, any walker stopped
by a curious friend and asked to look, to touch something
native but not common, unassuming, discreet,
of slight human use but entirely at home in its place.

American Hornbeam, *Carpinus caroliniana*

WHEN THE LONG-EAR VISITED

Michael Loderstedt

Under gray din, cold rain
we stand, shoulder to shoulder
masked, for glimpse of barred
feathers along spruce trunk.

A Long-Eared Owl
roosts here, photographers
murmur lens lengths
& owl wash.

They're posting uploads
of blurry captures, texting
coordinates as bluejays
screech alarm bells.

Impossible ears wave
thin orange flags in
faint sun, moth-like it
flutters from commotion.

In this wretched year
I cannot believe you exist
Long-Ear, that you'd stop
here in this wood
for us, for me.

Under mask, mouth
mumbles mother's camp song—
Do your ears hang low?
Do they wobble to and fro?

Can you tie 'em in a knot?
Can you tie them in a bow?
What say you, fine
gift of treetops?

Long-Eared Owl, *Asio otus*

White-Footed Mouse, *Peromyscus leucopus*

WHITE-FOOTED MICE IN WINTER, CLEVELAND, 2020

Michelle Skupski Bissell

I want to like these mice,
I do. For my 8-year-old son

and his mess of predator/
prey lines in science class.

I feel safe
in that web. The mice

are always at the bottom
like in 7th grade

when I reached into the dark
shelf of my locker

and fingered the cold
squish of the dead

mouse. I didn't want to
toss it in the trash

for the smell so I slid it
on my teacher's desk and

left. I wanted to leave
my unease there too,

the memory of a lost
mouse stumbling through

our kitchen when I was 12,
my little brother climbing

the kitchen table, screeching
because a mouse does not belong

here. I am not a natural predator.
I don't need

this mouse for anything and yet
here I am nearing my 38th year

still holding all these mice
close, squeezing. They scramble

around in my mind like
the many that foraged our attic

floorboards as I tried to sleep.
They won't let me

rest. And I wonder now
who or what is safe

and when. I have a house
and a door and a lock and

still I find another mouse
making a home

in my other son's roller skate,
soft padding for safety

of another kind. Mouse,
will you ever leave me

alone? Dearest Self,
you are safe in your mask

in your bubble with a broken
garage door and not enough

money for repair. Today
you will feed the birds.

Splendid Earth-Boring Beetle, *Geotrupes splendidus*

VARIATION ON WINGS

Kortney Morrow

Dazzling is a flash of green
bursting out from under an old leaf
      as dozens of iridescent insects
      scatter towards the sun.
Their metallic bodies holding
hidden wings. Six delicate legs
      skimming the soil, surrending
      to the decomposition of the earth.
Their ancient eyes looking at the rot
running through the forest floor and
      seeing possibility. Deep breaths
      are not a lung expanding in and out.
They are the air passing through
every opening of a body. To be
      wrapped up by the wind, to be
anchored in the ground.

MAYAPPLE'S SLOW DANCE

Rebecca Wohlever

Beckoned by lingering sun and the
footsteps of children,
Soft green parisoles ease their way through the fallen and fading
    love letters of autumn.
Turning slowly as they enter the forest dance floor,
chartreuse skirts unfurling,
stories of a long winter, once tucked into their folds, now exhale
    and surrender to warmth.

The fruit will swell and ripen in late summer.
Mothers will warn against eating the tempting egg-shaped
    treasures that dangle only from the two-leaved plants.

Until then, they are a tropical floor canopy, where young children
    pretend with toy soldiers and dolls.

Until then, a father leads his daughter past their lazy green lobes to
    the mossy banks of a fishing hole, where bluegill look up
    from their underwater world to waving streaks of sunshine.

A forest song leaves its words in an ear too young to understand
    and an ear too old to listen.

Lyrics are deer hooves sinking into soft spring ground,

Rootlets reaching their tender anchors into the mycelium,

Green-robed goddesses spinning into existence.

Melody is every winter dream that became a wildflower.

Rhythm is your own beating heart.

Mayapple, *Podophyllum peltatum*

Virginia Bluebells, *Mertensia virginica*

RESOUNDING THROUGH THE BRUSH & BRANCH

Bronlynn Thurman

Nestled amongst the dense undergrove
your sweet cacophony pierces through the monochrome
Vibrant clusters of raindrops sing
melancholy melodies

Yearning to burrow into your warm embrace
I seek reprieve from pervasive musings
My mortality hanging in the balance until
your presence calls forth slow, unfolding mornings

Wind whispering honeyed notes of desire
The ballad lifts from the loam and carries me forward

My love, I dream of the moment you unfurl
A sign of the times
Mertensia virginica
It's only right you bear the weight of this oath

And as the bell tolls
I'm left longing for warmer days

Hepatica, *Hepatica*

FIELD GUIDE TO FLEETING MOMENTS

Amanda Schuster

Dusted in pollen
a clumsy bumblebee lands
atop her petals:

Hepatica Nobilis,
ephemeral queen,
angel of fleeting moments:

The smell after rain
The spinal stretch of a cat
The sharp breath running uphill.

In the forest-floor opera,
everything singing,
Hepatica,
a whispered aria:

Let us return to the earth that made us.
Let us surrender to the sun again.
Let us feel the pulse in our knuckles
holding hands.

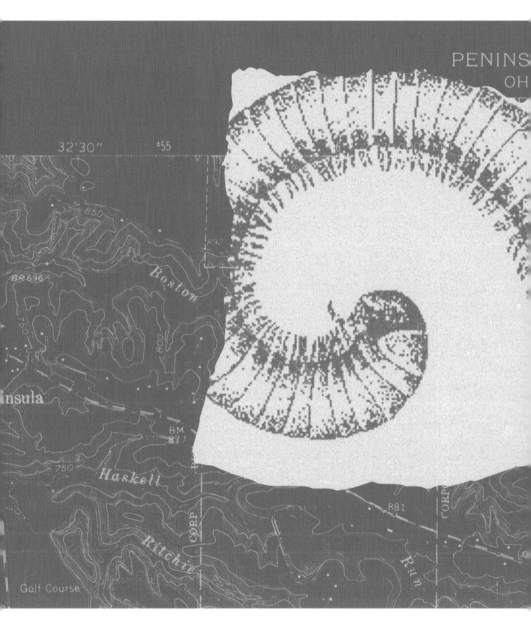

American Giant Millipede, *Narceus americanus*

AMERICAN GIANT MILLIPEDE

Mary Quade

Iron-red tube,
thick as a pinky
and often longer,
it undulates along the
forest floor in darkness,
cleaning up the dead.
Besides the legs, there's
nothing much to see, its
armor plain and shiny—
no wings, no spots, no
fleshy abdomen exposed,
no fateful stinger.
Only a snub head, short
antennae, waving, dull eyes
not seeming to see.
Not venomous,
unlike the centipede—
that flat biter hunting
in the basement.
But poisonous; when
unsettled, it curls up—
hard exoskeleton, a shield;
legs spooning legs—
and oozes yellow toxins,
untasty to a creature
seeking out a fat bug.
I'll admit, they unsettle
me a little, their constant
crawling, an iron train of

segments—on each: two pairs
of legs moving in waves
along the ground, grasping
at decay. I can barely
keep track of my own
two feet beneath me; every
stick, every rock, every mud
puddle—a potential stumbling.
Or worse, a fall. But a
millipede can't fall, except
further into earth, where
it builds a burrow to molt
into a new self, soft,
at first, then once again solid,
a larger thing which will
consume at least some of its
exuvia, its former skin.
Here is something, though:
when a female lays her egg,
for each she creates a pellet of
chewed plants and her feces,
where she entombs the egg,
then passes that pellet along
her legs into her anal valve,
which closes on the tiny
wet nest, drying it in the kiln
of her body, until it emerges
a hard ball, both a shell
and a hatchling's meal.
What measures we all
will take to make
a future.

THAT TIME I FOUND A STAR IN MY BACKYARD

Isaiah Hunt

I was sitting outside on the porch while Mama and her man bickered in the living room about God-knows-what. My hands were still greasy from her baked chicken, with half a bottle of Thunder Punch glowing bright at my side, its lemony aftertaste on my tongue. It was below freezing, but the heated argument seemed enough to keep me warm. I distracted myself counting what little snowfall I could.

97 . . .

　　98 . . .

　　　　99 . . .

On the hundredth snowflake, a yellow-ish green hue similar to my Thunder Punch twinkled in the dark. I squinted at what looked like a chocolate chip chilling on a big snow cone, but instead was a black bug looking lost in all the white, using a beacon to phone home. I edged closer, hovering my smallest and least greasy finger over its shell, and its legs latched right onto the tip of my nail. I nearly freaked out, expecting its light as a weapon to burn through my skin, or use its alien-like glow to teleport me a thousand miles away into its spaceship. Still hearing Mama's voice thrash about inside, I wouldn't have minded the latter. But it wiggled its antennae in an attempt to communicate with me. *I come in peace.* Although I couldn't understand its words, leaving it alone in the cold didn't sit right with me, so I brought it inside, the bug's butt still aglow. I wondered about the flavor of its light. Lemon? Sour Apple? Maybe banana. I ushered it into an empty hairspray bottle while I unlocked my tablet and asked Alexa about this strange creature.

I'd come in contact with one of the few firefly species left on Earth: A winter firefly, one of the many victims of what people call the light wars, because our phones, streets, houses and cars pollute the planet with their light, as if in competition to burn brighter than the Sun. Discovering one in my backyard had to be a miracle.

I swiped through my tablet to learn more, my eight-year-old brain a predator for new information. Destroyed forests meant little to no homes for these delicate critters, and the fireflies who survived were now being abducted, their light harvested for glow-in-the-dark food and drinks to sell in stores.

My heart sank at one of these drinks' names.

Thunder Punch! Awaken the lightning inside.

I stared at their website. Strawberry-flavor pulsed in a bubblegum pink. Blueberry-flavor radiated in sky blue. Lemon in neon yellow. A tremendous amount of guilt washed over me. So that's where they had gone. In my belly.

Yet, there were countless forums dedicated to reverting to the days where backyards would be full of fireflies.

Rekindle with the fireflies!

Remember fireflies?

Shut off your lights, make room for the fireflies!

A Comprehensive Guide to Bringing Back the Fireflies.

I miss the fireflies.

This was the side I wanted to join.

No more Thunder Punch from the corner store, I promised myself as I rummaged through the kitchen for an empty and clear sugar jar. I stole a rose from Mama's bouquet that her man would offer as an apology, since I thought the firefly needed a reminder of home. I watched it land on the rose's cane within the jar and blink its light with delight. I was learning its love language. Mama had found out, but she didn't mind. Fireflies are a sign to slow down and cherish the small things, she said. And that, I did. I felt like I made friends with a tiny star.

It felt refreshing to have someone who didn't spend their time arguing or poke fun at my dreams, even if we were from two different worlds. Amidst other second graders who bounced in their seats, hands raised, shouting to be influencers, professional gamers, and streamers, I was the kid in the back who thought being an astronaut would be cool. Faces scrunched in and chuckled; an astronaut didn't sound fun, but it was fitting for the kid who usually sat alone in their own space, smacking on leftover baked chicken and unknowingly sipping on firefly juice. When I eventually told Mama about my astronaut ambitions, and she only whispered, "that's nice," with a slight twitch in her smile, that dream flickered out. It didn't matter; my purpose in life was reignited. A protector of the fireflies.

That was until one day I had done the unforgivable.

Earlier that morning, I overslept after another late-night dispute between Mama and her man and missed the bus. I wanted to tell her I'd rather stay home, because I really didn't feel like feeling lonely at school that day, but Mama's Chevy was already honking outside. She was late for work, but I was desperate to find my tablet. I switched on my ceiling light and found it from underneath a pile of unhung clothes. Mama's horn blasted again, and I fled out the house.

Hours later when I returned home to my starry friend, my ceiling was still bursting with light. My friend's light, completely extinguished.

Imagine entering the world as an adult, prepared to share your rare talent only to realize everyone—even their food—performs your talent so much better. You've been outshined, so you hide what you believed was your unique gift from this universe, hoping one day it's needed again. I think that's the real reason winter fireflies lose their light. My friend's beady eyes gazed up at my brightened room and probably thought, *what's the point?*

But Alexa assured me that winter fireflies lose their ethereal glow slowly after reaching adulthood. That didn't make me feel any better. I trapped the majority of my friend's life inside a jar as something to talk about my day, to cuddle with when Mama and her man got to yelling again, or use it as a simple night light to keep me from complete darkness.

At the exact spot we met, I opened the jar. It fluttered from its slightly withered rose before blasting off and blending in with the night, never to be seen again. I felt heartbroken at how quickly it chose to leave with no time to say goodbye, but in hindsight, I understand.

Sometimes, when I'm relaxing on my own porch with a cup of hot chocolate, I wonder about what became of that winter firefly. I hope no other silly kid tried to catch it. I hope it didn't find itself in someone's drink. I hope with the remainder of its life, it found a family to love.

If I could speak with you again, my little star, I'd say we need you. Forget about the streetlights, tablets, our luminescent drinks. You're the most authentic kind of light we'll witness in our lifetime. I know a thousand roses won't make up for the destruction of your kin, but please rest knowing the dozens of winter fireflies who've now taken refuge in the groves of my backyard are not alone.

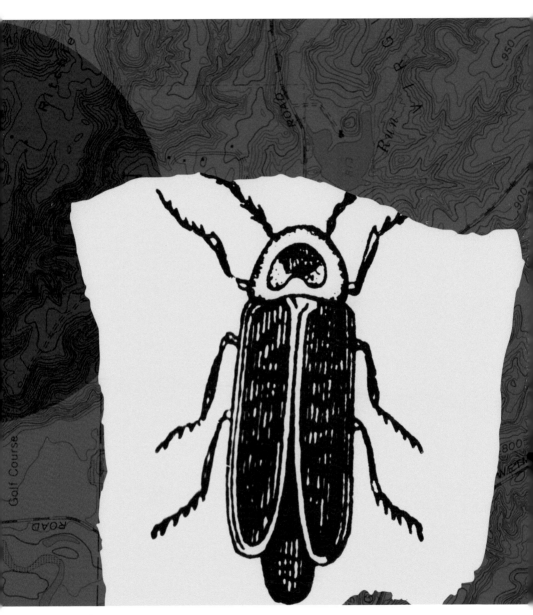

Winter Firefly, *Ellychnia corrusca*

Eastern Screech Owl, *Megascops asio*

A RAY OF MIDNIGHT SUNSHINE

Dr. R. Ray Gehani

Midnight moon peeks
Eastern screeching owl turns head
My insomniac companions.

Big Brown Bat, *Eptescius fuscus*

I NEED GLASSES FOR MY EARS.

Sujata Lakhe

Listen
sonic waves
entering your cochlea
stimulating your ear cilia
could conjure up an image
play a movie on the screen of your mind
                              of a fleeting moth.

Imagine
ears were sending signal
to optical lobes
a shape of an object
its density
its velocity
and at any given second
where the object
is in the context of a room, rendering
Light irrelevant.

Bat-shit crazy, don't you think?

Big Brown Bat is making
Her own light, but her light
Is sound. She opens wide
her chihuahua mouth
to let an Edvard Munch's
scream from deep inside,
bouncing, echoing, infinite.

Inaudible to human but heard
by many creatures

Anthropocentric compulsions
interpret bared fangs as anger,
nocturnal activities as evil and blind.
We need a receiver-in-the-ear,
that slows down her long,
complex song over 45
Hertz into a boring,
chip . . . chip . . . chip, like
slow-motion film, a song
not simply to make silent
objects speak and thus avoid
stalagmites but to hunt,
locate to kill to consume.

Light-less air fills
with sparks of sound
her echolocating brain drops a pin,
she moves with precise
homing device,
catabolic fire in her belly
engulfing the midge mid-flight.

Bats and humans, kin
from time immemorial, whether
standing on two feet
or hanging by the claws
whether in a pre-historic cave
or an Ohio National Forest, they
live in the same home

looking out of different windows
lost in our own sensory foam.

Can we human ever know
what it is like to be a bat?

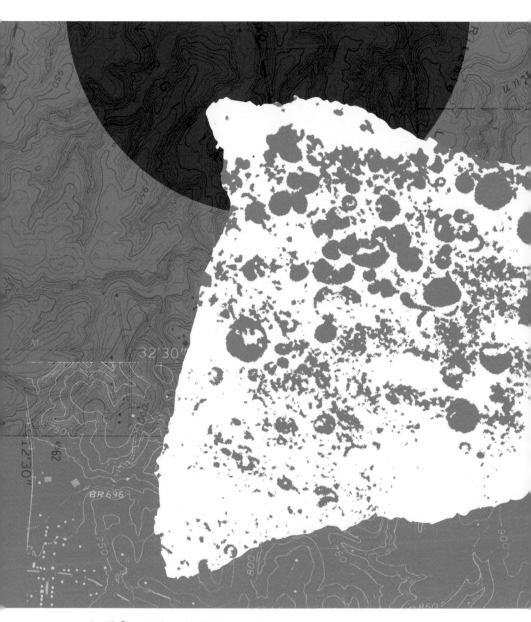

Candleflame Lichen, *Candelaria concolor*

CANDLEFLAME LICHEN
Clara Britton

I love you I love you I love you
I want to live on you love in you
Let us find a tree, and settle down
you can take the sun
and I will make the fruit
When I first found you
years ago (maybe longer now)
I saw us painting yellow
over the places they called barren
I saw us swallowing the heavy things
they could no longer carry

Now, after knowing you wrapped in my lungs,
I understand that this is our burden for a good life
so full of copper and mercury
we will never go hungry

They call you names I would never
let you hear. I say
photobiont
meaning: light eater,
color inside me. Meaning: life saver,
couldn't do this without you,
look at what we've made
I spread for you on this bark bed,
golden laced gratitude, look how I spread for you.

AN ARTIST'S BRACKET

Susann Moeller

I wish I had your
cosmopolitan distribution, dear.
While no one has you for lunch,
some will have you for tea.

And so, this poet raises
her *Scarlet Cup* to
the pungent inspiration
in these odorous woods.

I waltz through mycology,
where *Turkey Tails* and
Hens in the Woods
flock without feathers;

where moss and lichen
cover and layer the playground
of rotting bones, leaves, and scat
for Hänsel & Gretel and Snow White.

Beneath my feet
spreads a carpet of hosts
to Saprophytes,
Biophytes and Necrophytes.

Beer and cheese need them
as much as I crave you.
You, neither plant nor animal
but part of Thoreau's lore!

As I walk on *Silky Parchment*,
stroking in passing a *Lion's Mane*,
Funeral Bells chime from afar
and in the *Dryad's Saddle*

that hung from an oak nearby,
or was it a maple—I ride
through the Grimm brothers' tales
and dash away from parasites

on logs and stumps and pale gleams
that hide amatoxin under
their white satin skirts
and promise the *Death Angel's Kiss.*

Artist's Bracket, *Ganoderma applanatum*

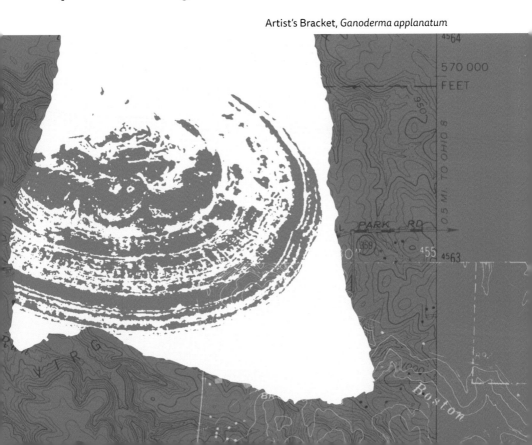

Sugar Maple, *Acer saccharum*

UPON LEARNING THAT DOUBLE SAMARAS ALSO LITTER THE HEAVENS

Steve Brightman

And it's not enough
to know sugar maples
have lined the banks
of Lake Erie since
before Christ literally
or figuratively
walked the earth.
And it's not enough
to feel the sweetened
cool of their canopy
as they blacken the sun
above the luscious
gurgle of the Cuyahoga.
And it's barely enough
    —just barely—
to heap young belief
upon young belief that
they are angel wings
helicoptering from the
Ohio sky just for you.

ARION FUSCA

Ray McNiece

Consider the Northern Dusky Slug—
doubt you ever have, except "ew".
Never have camouflage stripes moved so

slowly as it slimes across the arm
of the Adirondack chair riding its
ancient ocean wave secreted

from lone rippling foot. The Dusky
differs from other Arions in the yellow
orange body mucus in case you

haven't noticed, nor does it
contract into a bell shape when
stimulated—not that you'd try.

A shell-less terrestrial mollusk,
would we trust this world as we
go about so naked? The pneumostome

blow hole sucks the burning air
into the long tube of its single lung,
thick viscous breathing sleeve.

It's been slugging along this way
for millenia, no doubt sliming a dead
dinosaur's ass, and now this chair arm—

just another rotting log as far

as it's concerned. Slow and steady
wins the race in the land of decay

and regeneration from primordial muck
that we keep our distance from there at the edge
of swamp oaks leaning, trying not to fall.

Northern Dusky Slug, *Arion fuscus*

Japanese Honeysuckle, *Lonicera japonica*

A LOST LETTER FROM A TREE TO THE JAPANESE HONEYSUCKLE

Shei Sanchez

You wring my breath away.

To feel your million ovaline lips,
    leaves of emerald cascading

up and down my spine. To feel you
    twine tight around me, tendrils

a tender corset of cellulose divine.
    To wake in the spring smelling

your nectar's sweat on my neck,
    a siren's attar lulling me to yield.

You are a slippery dancer cradling
    my hips with petals of silver

and gold, an unfinished poem seeking
    to dazzle my timid heart, a pirate ship

forever moored to the base of my throat.

Barred Owl, *Strix varia*

BARRED OWL RHAPSODY

Courtney Noster

I met your essence first
next to the pond
nestled in between the winding vine and that tree.

It was surprising when I saw it.
Warmth veined across my soma.
I reached to touch your banded feather
suspended there, deliberately it seemed.

All at once in that moment,
nature communing,
I was totally in love.
Caressed by the downy
of the winged-sublime,

your feather
my skin

connected.

Lifetimes of our acquaintance remembered
that early spring day.

I learned you next by sound
in the language of vibration
echoing from the hollows where you live.

I heard you calling in a lover's song
a courtship duet across the creek.

While lake waves murmured in the distance
you were caterwauling with another,
crooning to the moon.
Your sounds were wild and playful, monkey-like
and I heard you wondering who's cookin' for who.

Serenaded by your forest vernacular,
I listened carefully
with ears as wide open as
your obsidian eyes.

Just as the sailor is evolved by the siren's song
I was different when you stopped singing,
and I wondered when we'd meet again?

Until that sunny day in January
against a periwinkle sky.
When I finally came to know you again, by sight.

There you were sitting earnestly
in the center, a singing hollow
in an old Sycamore tree.
Gently atop of it all
in the middle of the crown spread
while crystal sunlight basked you
outlining your rounded head.
You were a vision
amongst the gleaming white, mottled branches
with which you effortlessly merged.

Even from far away, on the ground
I could see your steady ways.
Your head swishing softly one direction to the next

and I wondered what you could see.
Wondered if you saw me.

I stood quietly, dried leaves underfoot, in your presence until
an adoring observer with a long lens noticed me
noticing you.
She took your picture and showed me your features up close.
Your yellow beak and winking eye I'll never forget.
Our spiritual acquaintance was forged.

That photo now adorns my nest, the place I call home
everytime I see it
I say thank you, gentle sentinel of the forest
for all the ways you are love.

GRAY CATBIRD ON THE NEST

Theresa Göttl Brightman

If you hear a mewling cry, between a
human child and a disappointed cat,
in the dense shrubs of your yard,

and see a flash of rust
under a handful-cloud of slate gray,
leave her be.

She is friendly but shy, transitory,
fierce in defense.
If you could ask her,

she would tell you
she does nothing heroic.
It is what her people do.

One thousand miles,
from south to north then south again,
following budding trees in the spring

to a fresh hold of twigs in the undergrowth
where she raises her babies
and fights off blue jays and grackles.

And when the brown-headed cowbird
gets up to the old cuckoo tricks,
her sharp, dark eye watches.

She jabs the intruder's eggs
and rolls them from the nest.
She knows invasion.

She does not proceed with irrational fury.
   Nor does she ignore the threat,
waiting until danger blossoms and fruits.

She acts, protecting
the innocents in her care, and ends
the parasite incursion before it begins.

She would tell you
she does nothing heroic.
It is what her people do.

Gray Catbird, *Dumatella carolinensis*

DON'T EAT THE FLOWERS YOU SHOULDN'T

Chad W. Lutz

I imagine
tasting the
sanguinarine
as my eyes
bite into the
reddish stem
of this white
flowering
plant

but don't let
its pretty yellow
stamens fool you

someone told me
eating too much
of it can kill you

alkaloids in the
rhizomes & roots

it makes sense

when you get
to the root of things
there is poison

circulating like
vinyl chloride

in the soil
throughout the
watersheds
in our bodies

things we regret
things we tire of

and yet
here lies hope
in a poisonous
flower

looking pretty
enough to take another picture

Bloodroot, *Sanguinaria canadensis*

American Chestnut, *Castanea dentata*

BLIGHT OF THE AMERICAN CHESTNUT

Carrie George

with observations from the naturalist Donald Culross Peattie

The chestnut grows blighted and destined to die
on the bodies of giants that once feathered and bloomed
like a sea with white combers plowing across its surface.

Illness inhabits a legacy, inhabits a system
of root, trunk, and vein swirling through
the chestnut, grown blighted and destined to die.

Browns resurrect in lovely women's locks,
in fine silk cuts pleated into dresses, curtains, tablecloths
like seas with white combers plowing across the surface.

Resurrected in memory and laboratories where needles
shock cankers into surviving samples. We play god
on the chestnuts, growing blighted and destined to die

or to try, at least. Generational loops curse roots back
into fatal sprouts with only distant dreams of parents
like a sea with white combers plowing across its surface.

We treasured their wood in pianos, barn timbers, fences,
smoothed their tall torsos into human shapes and desires.
The blighted chestnut we sentenced to drown
its white combers still bobbing on the surface.

Masked Bees, *Hylaeus*

A SAFFRON PRISM

Zach Savich

I like a yard of anything
not grass / milkweed asters carrot
blossoms the thistle-rose / saffron
calms them / just
enough / as highway runoff
ices ditches / or snow
falling fast enough
to dry the sheets / and masked
bees carrying snow
like pollen / fast enough
it dries by when they reach the hive

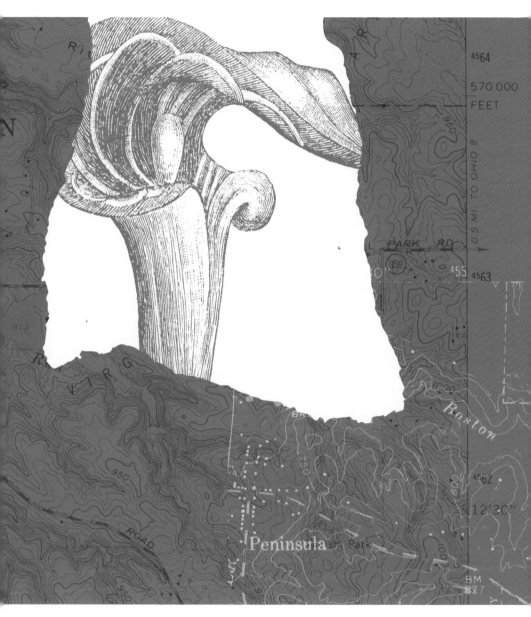

Jack-in-the-Pulpit, *Arisaema triphylum*

JACK-IN-THE-PULPIT
Michael Buebe

present
    for your presentation
       your wrapping
    green cloth   of any
          simple fabric

peaking for congress
    for the first
    calming breath

    (vulnerable / in breathing / in filling your lungs)

before the sermon

       & then

     (!)
        the word of silence
        is passed
           in turn
              plant to plant
                 &
              gnat to gnat

(so serene the lesson
the sun & silence)

Poison Ivy, *Toxicodendron radicans*

POISON IVY

Marina Vladova

Lingering idly in an open field or well-worn path,
with hairy growth along a downed or standing tree
emergent leaflets, shapes of three subopposite,
oblong and pointed, toothed and smooth
a subtle single notch or deeply lobed
with pearl-shaped fleshy fruit
she feeds the birds and spreads the seeds
She grows from pliant fragments in the ground
Takes root where stems touch soil
On human skin her oily drop of pinprick's range—The oozy itch
reminds us that we never left the serpent's garden.

THE EASTERN RED-BACKED SALAMANDER

Tovli Simiryan

Another note, you hiking alone,
in/out of cyber-space near some campsite in West Virginia,
moving slowly along a nameless creek, eventually closing in on
Ohio.
So I print . . . so I have paper thoughts now,
folded for weeks inside my LL Bean kangaroo pocket,
a soft hunk of fluff; not the brittle leaves you crush as
fall arrives beneath your boots, dust filling cavities—
something to guess at . . . or, better still, declare humbling.
Just send me a picture—the Red-backed Salamander, for example,
before it forms a crust against leaves and gravel.
I hear its red striped skin is forever—a tattoo of belonging,
social monogamy and defended homelands.
Sounds like something you're looking for, doesn't it?
Anyway, I've stopped guessing, or better still everything I own
is an envelope licked, sealed shut and tasted—the hollow places
filled
with living beings, or some plastic bottle tossed aside, now part of
a tattooed reptile's habitat. Everything has its little place whether
discarded,
remembered or born . . .
that's it, birth; I am born deeper and deeper
and looking up, there are so many eyes, so many suns—
every piece the darkened forest transcending an upheaval of
principle,

the little creek with no name and, then your footprints floating against the water;
spinning in the air. There you are—drowning in the earth; hanging on precariously of course—see how much we've loved you?

Eastern Red-Backed Salamander, *Plethodon cinereus*

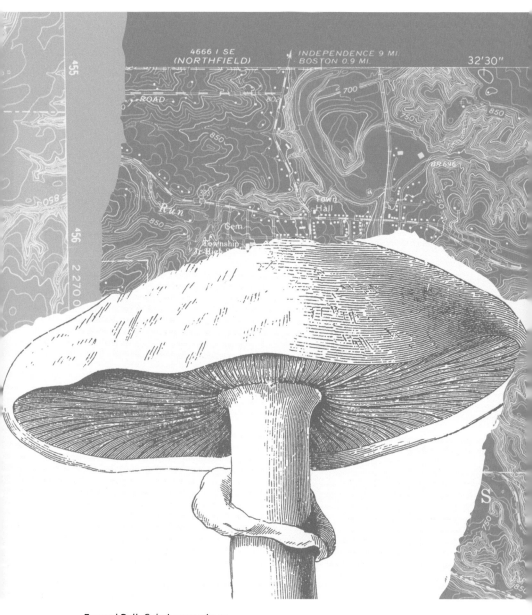

Funeral Bell, *Galerina marginata*

FUNERAL BELLS
Tishon Woolcock

late. the edge of fall

at every step funeral bells

we pull from the dry leaves what we can

we hope we won't go hungry

though what we carry might kill us

a cool air signals the creek

our cities long gone

all that's left to settle is ahead

III Rivers, Lakes, Ponds, and Wetlands

Star Jellies, *Nostoc*

STAR JELLY
Cameron Gorman

then the meteors came, and they left us.

we fell down from some bright place, blanketed
the grass, the branches, the thing we called sleep.

nobody knows how we eat sunbeams,
where we go when the rain stops.
they call us remains. they call us earth-star.

they have tried to name us. we were uligo,
which meant fat from the earth,
a star which has fallen.

we remember the atmosphere, its dizzy wash
of blue-beams. the streaming before we were
star-slubber, star-slough, caca de luna.

we remember fire, the heat close to heaven.
the coldness that could not touch us.

the showers came, and they carried us down,
and we became your star-shot, and we became
translucent, which means allowing some light
to pass through.

North American River Otter, *Lontra canadensis*

OTTER THEOLOGY

Anastasios Mihalopoulos

One of the all-pro cool animals—no real enemies except
us, a nutty sense of humor, bad-ass musculature and maritime
skills. Otters rock.
    —Brian Doyle

We play games
like the samaras spinning overhead,
spiraling to some far-off place
never taking root.
And what of roots,
of rivers and their beds?
We cannot sleep
without each other.
The grounding of
one hand in another.
But first, this cacophony,
this game of hunt and catch.
Sift, splash, squeal
when she bites too hard
then paddle fast,
feel the undulation
of body and torso, of hip and tail.
Cool hue, rushing under your belly
Water, clear as sun.
Feel naked in the shade.
Hardly any of us remain,
go on playing anyways.

American White Water Lily, *Nymphaea odorata*

AMERICAN WATERLILY

Geoffrey Polk

Out of the muck of Northeast Ohio
    out of the Cuyahoga valley
out of this mud-clotted shallow pond
    bordered by towpath and scenic railroad
jogged past by runners, bicycle sprinters,
    strollers and Sunday photographers,
interrupted periodically by sound blasts
    to scare crows from corn fields,
they appeared one day on the pond's surface,
    launched from pie-sliced pads of green,
apparitions out of the mist, creamy yellow and white,
    floating aliens whose startling glow,
mesmerizing and canyon-deep,
    stops the meadow traffic in its tracks,
binoculars fluttering, camera lenses shattered,
    walkers fainting, bikes piled together,
dogs slumped to the ground, birds cloister-silent.
    The flowers opening, spreading,
dimpling the still pond, fragrant petals,
desired by muskrats, radially symmetric,
they emerge from module Earth like space walkers
    tethered to pond bottom
by branched root rhizomes, rising along long petioles,
    umbilicals holding these comets of wonder
for us to see, mirrors of our soul—
    we, aloft, adrift, waiting for the message
to call us home.

Water-Forget-Me-Not, *Myosotis scorpioides*

REMEMBER-YOU-WILL-DIE SUN

Alyssa Perry

Myosotis scorpioides, the false memory or sun you are yet
here with me, once wooded once seed, is of the borages
who don't relate to each other like we do.

It arrived in Europe and Asia, having been narrowly
plucked from nowhere, including rarely North America, as
a native species and forever garden pleasantry. The plant was
infrequent, on narrow stilts in Britain, however it
was very there in Jersey. [3]

It was lost unusually in arid and desertified habitat, though
not found in steppe, dune, tundra, roadway, hill or
concrete. If it scorned dry water, it would perish in sky's emergence
and could render dissolute the firm flying-up foundations.

It was a crouched and descending thing no less than 70 cm,
receiving large (8–12 mm) fruit, pinks let go
when partially closed, yellow in full bloom, with blue outside
and milk to follow. Animal of the ubiquitous brief stigma.
The roots were linear to oblong,

menopausal up top. From first frost to midspring it
flourished in extreme. How I'll miss you is not known

This poem uses material from the Wikipedia article "Myosotis scorpioides," modified from
the original.

Banded Fishing Spider, *Dolomedes vittatus*

FISHING SPIDER
Charles Malone

You meet her, among the cracks
and right angles of Deep Lock Quarry.

She crabs back to cover her clutch of eggs.

Your muscles go taut in the same way
wild, and unconsidered—heart quick
without enough breath to compare
your relative mass, you back away.

I tell you she can prey on fish five times her body size
just to turn your blood on. Pumping too loud in your ears to consider
    her family: the nursery web spiders
—a different way to name her.

I wonder what is/isn't automatic or natural?

We ought to be careful, looking over the menu at Fisher's Cafe,
that no one decides to name us by what we consume:

Bread people, beef people, egg crushers & cheese melters, oil folks & forest
eaters, mountain top destroyers, those who confuse shame for power—
then swallow it all, drainers of rivers, desert makers, 73 hot dogs in 10
minutes, entire neighborhoods of old homes, feeding on memory, feeding
on self-improvement, clutching our eggs & our pets close to the tangle of
veins & arteries & nerves in our core, web of ribs, sternum & carapace.

Common Green Darner, *Anax junius*

DANCE OF THE GREEN DARNERS

Marion Starling Boyer

Half my head is eyes
so I see you behind me

whizzing to capture a gnat.
I whir and you whip near.

Thirty thousand facets
of your green eyes fasten on me.

You hover, glassy wings fanning,
thorax beating. The turquoise

of your abdomen dazzles.
I offer my head to your clasp

and in tandem we wing
through sheen and shadow,

skimming water, skimming air
until I swing my tail up,

curl to grasp your bright blue
in the basket of my legs.

We hold each other in the wheel
and the world spins

blueandgreen until I forget
any history before you.

Spring Peeper, *Pseudacris crucifer*

ODE TO SPRING, PEEPER

Barbara Sabol

Through your frozen sleep, dreams
of beetles, of robin song, of mud-sweet air,
of what passes for love at the wetland's edge.

After a slow thaw, your heart resumes its lusty rhythm
and you rustle awake in your snug of dead leaves
under a fallen log.

Small as a child's thumb, piercing as a night train,
you stir the woods back to what you sing for—
another spring.

So begins the boreal forest song. Elsewhere
ice caps weep into the sea; waters warm
and rise
                              yet now

this enormous chorus, a hallelujah
of miniature bells, beckons me out
to the moon-struck backyard.

American Bullfrog, *Lithobates catesbeianus*

WINTER WALK

Laura Grace Weldon

Pavement icebound, I walk instead
around the pond, notice my steps attend
to a circle's beginning and end while
animals, free of fence or cage, attend differently.

Their tracks follow hollows and ridges,
scents and sounds, a hundred variables beyond
my wavelength, all stories I will never know.

Water wrestled into ice heaves at the bank
grasps winter-softened leaves, reeds gone brittle.
The willow's knuckled roots clutch at the edge,
branches leafed with tiny birds fluttering into flight.

Secrets, unseen, surround me. Blanding's turtles,
bluegill, American bullfrogs sleep deep in the pond's lungs
as I pass. Snakes, salamanders, dragonfly nymphs
wait nearby for spring. They know this icy landscape's
promise. I haven't yet mastered such faith.

COMMON PAWPAW

Isaiah Back-Gaal

for Vicky

We were so sure of ourselves. Time
after time turning leaves to measure

the relative degree of waxiness against
the three-pronged symmetry of their veins,

photosynthetic power as a principle of green
warmth. We were always wrong.

So adept at identifying the incorrect
tree, which is to say we introduced ourselves

to strangers and still received bashful
rustling. What did we do to deserve

such patience? Friend, you are deep morning
breaths and hefty breakfasts. Your limbs arc

towards secure and fertile ground. The woods
are a disco for your dancing and someone is there,

calling out your name, which echoes,
which means you have never been

alone. Someone wraps you in lace
to hold your blooms, which, red and heavy

as a well-worn organ, hang downwards.
Do they ring out to the grieving earth

below, to a beetle, to a lover, standing just
a little ways off? Did you know, scientists call

this kind of flower *perfect?* Light enters
the grove. We leave with only each other,

and a glimpse of a future overcome with fruit.

Common Pawpaw, *Asimina triloba*

Common Garter Snake, *Thamnophis sirtalis*

THE COMMON GARTER SNAKE

Caitie Young

at the foot of my grandmother's garden bed
hidden in wild mint and the remains of last years azaleas
i find you
with the setting sun reflecting the shine on your belly
as yellow as the dandelion heads i've rubbed on my arm
your verdant armor could not shield you as you treat yourself
to slugs and earthworms, all the pests scurrying
through cattails guarding the creek
it's minutes before i know you're dead
and your life slithering through weeds
in the garden is over before the ripple in the water finds the shore

Jacob's Ladder, *Polemonium reptans*

STAIRWAY TO HEAVEN: JACOB'S LADDER

Risha Nicole

Heavenly foliage,
your sweet roots
spread and captivate the soil
of my grandmother's
garden.
She kneels and weeds
away at her thoughts,
with the hope
of being free enough
to climb your stairway.
She cares for you,
and you grant well wishes.
Hiding away from the sun,
your leaves tend to scorch
under the warmness of day.
Your stems rise
and threaten
to touch Heaven.

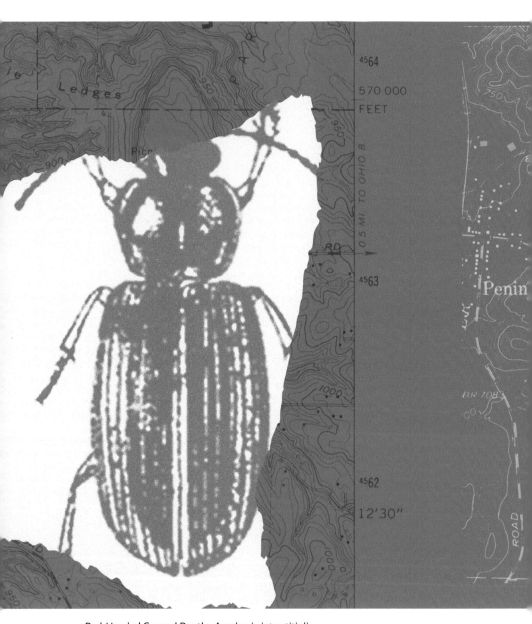

Red-Headed Ground Beetle, *Amphasia interstitialis*

UPON SEEING A RED-HEADED GROUND BEETLE I'VE DECIDED: I'M MORE ABOUT PROTECTION OF THE WEAK THAN I AM SURVIVAL OF THE FITTEST

Bob King

Most of what we do, directly or indirectly,

is about distracting us from the fact that

we'll all be dead soon. We're all just renters.

But maybe it's also about being remembered

after we're kaput. Squished. Entombed. See also:

headstones and mausoleums, which really

are just fancy Post-it Notes for the future

generations for when they walk through

the field-cemetery-kitchen of our past lives:

we hope they see the hasty scribble and forgive

us for eating all the plums in the icebox which

they were probably saving but were so delicious

and sweet and we simply couldn't help

ourselves. Don't be a plum eater. Think of

others. Conserve. Learn trivia along the trail:

Did you know Darwin's Galopagoan boat

was called the *Beetle?* Wait. That's not true.

It was the *Beagle.* But I misheard the podcast

or the lyrics and thought John, Paul, and George

might've been trying to make some kind of evolved

statement after the hard days and nights in Hamburg,

where their 10,000 hours of play transformed them

from amateurs into experts. But no. They weren't

naturalists or activists. Yet. Did you know that

Neanderthals were most likely gingers—red tufted

and freckled and soulless and Germanic with limited

language but urgent with their *hubba hubba* eyebrow

arches in their pastoral pickup joints because

procreation. Because without procreation they

knew that the Homo sapiens on their way from

Africa would try to exterminate or assimilate or both.

Most of us still have at least 2% Neanderthal DNA.

That's a fact, you post-extinction caveman. Red yarn

red yarn red yarn—butterfly effect—and like an amateur

detective I can red yarn from Ethiopia to Hamburg

to the Cuyahoga Valley National Park and red yarn

from my footfalls on the crushed limestone towpath

to a quick scamper off-route and after taking a leak

beside a walnut tree like my epically aged ancestors,

like an expert I bend to check out the Red-Headed

Ground Beetle feasting on aphids just outside

Szalay's sweet corn field. Yes, it's true that this

ginger beetle is capable of mixing chemicals

in her dual pygidial glands—her butt—yes, in

her marvelous ass she can blend fluid and create

a combustion engine and POP! hot acrid gas

ejects and is capable of paralyzing even a small

mammal, like a shrew, which is why some beetles

are called bombardier beetles and even Darwin

got bombed by one, but that's not what took him

out. No. He was run over by a Volkswagen Bug

in the ironies to end ironies because like Alanis

Morissette, it's not ironic. And it's not true.

The Bug wasn't invented until about 50 years

after Darwin's ticker stopped, and even

the combined idea and design of Ferdinand

Porsche and Adolph Hitler couldn't have

resurrected a father of evolution, which—

red yarn—can be easily corrupted,

like anything, because as good as we are

at discovery and invention, our penchant

for perversion and exploitation of a good idea

is just as strong. See evolution. See eugenics.

See entomology. See deforestation. See politics.

See coup d'état. But the truth also is that Red-

Headed Beetles are beneficial creatures, despite

their incredible capacity for cruelty. Cruelty

isn't the point. For them. For us. Even the smallest

creatures make the globe spin like good vinyl.

And when all the broken-hearted people—broken

by the bullies and belligerent coaches and teachers

and family members and cliquey kids in a field

with a weaponized magnifying glass—yes,

when *all the broken-hearted people living in*

the world agree—agree that there's more power

in being a cheerleader than there is being a critic—

there will be an answer. Yes, there will be an answer.

Great Blue Heron, *Ardea herodias*

A GREAT BLUE HERON

Dan Dorman

After Christian died
I walked the Cuyahoga
To read haiku
And think

I saw him
In the water—

good bye

just

to   say

come   down   to   the   earth

A
g   r
e   t
a
b l
u
e

h
r   e
o n

Snapping Turtle, *Chelydra serpentina*

THE SNAPPING TURTLE

Jessica Jewell

I was born on top,
too hot for the nest.

I had eighty-eighty babies
on a railroad track.

I know rumbling & threat
that feeds in the fog

for months on end.
& the crush of sun

I visited once, & the eye
I lost to the bog.

THE MUSKRAT MAKES HIS BED

Catherine Wing

To the man who asked what I am good for,
a few words. It's true my ancestral name
is unfortunate—two rough things unkindly
brought together—but while you can't speak it,
musk is my language and rat's the size of my tongue.
Also, my ambition. What you don't know
would fill my burrow and its underwater entrance
twice over. With my extraordinary lung capacity
and my glossy underparts I made *Hinterlands Who's Who.*
In 2012, it was my famous lodge, den, and bed,
that earned me Wetland Designer of the Year.

It's true I eat sedge and cattail.
It's true I lap up pondweed and duck potato,
bulb and tuber, and if forced
I will stoop to snail and salamander.
It's true I am swamp and bog inclined.
I'm not picky.

My family's ancient and well-represented
in the fossil record. I am rumored to be descended
from the Balkan Snow Vole with whom I share a molar.
I can swim backwards and I can hold my breath
for a full 17 minutes. Are you good for that?

I am not a beaver and I am not a rat.
Call me what you will but I am native.
How rich for you, destroyer of habitats,
to accuse me of destructiveness, to blame me

for your leaking pond. I understand
that you think yours is the only story to tell
and that your way is the only way to tell it
but I have news for you.

Musk is how I sing, talk, love, woo, and warn.
It is my sign of bigger things yet to come.
You can't ice me over or push me out.
I will defend my bed, my burrow, and my craft.
Afterall who among us in this world
is not born blind and furless, given a name
by others and called to account?

Muskrat, *Ondatra zibethicus*

DAMSELS OF THE POND

Lindsay Barba

Damsels of the pond,
they say.
But we are the few who dare
to arrive first
at earliest sign of spring,
and carry on till hardest frost,
to be caught
waterside
perching upon
stems, twigs
in search of
our one love,
hearts as large
as the hawks
we once rivaled
in size.

We've warmed over
since those pre-
historic times.
Our radiant nymph bodies
born in a blaze of orange,
withering into powder
blue as our skin
dries in the high Ohio
summer sun, split
open at the head
to reveal
our muted hue.

Do not misconstrue
our name,
our soft bodies,
for innocence.
Instead, watch
closely—as we lurk,
wait
for our prey
and do a favor for
you hikers,
who confuse us for
our fire-breathing brethren,
devouring
the dreaded mosquito's head
in one bite.

Eastern Forktail, *Ischnura verticalis*

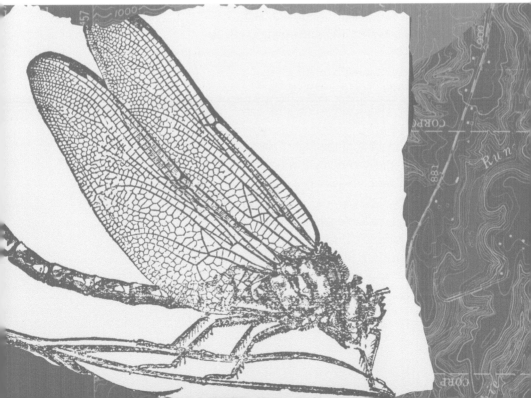

WOOD DUCK AUBADE

Diana Lueptow

It's a long drop. Night toward day
where mother waits, that first love
and commander. How deeply does

an animal dream? On jump day
she calls to earth. Thirty feet up
day-old hatchlings launch on small nerve;

untrained experts of resistance
they shape the air they cannot fly:
passage from night, anti-plummet—

a dream dispersing? Gravity
met half way, molecules flicked back,
air flow trimmed, webs and winglets bent,

sky divers shaping free fall. Drag,
to survivable speed—under
a minute, clutch of twelve down safe.

Watchman what of the night? Nestling,
sleeping, the watery night where
instinct rises and never sets.

The wood duck, a dabbling kind, nips
sedge, water lily. Ducklings can
walk on pads. A plunge unmanaged

would crack the sound barrier, hit

leaf mold like slamming on concrete.
The beaver pond—still. Outlandish

in his pied coats the drake swivels
a red eye, feathers aglow in
emerald flames, cobalt flames, sky

a summer cauldron of sunrise
on the marsh, perching nests in trees,
dappled water, a soft landing.

Wood Duck, *Aix sponsa*

Painted Turtle, *Chrysemys picta*

SUN LOVERS
Rebekah Ainsworth

I look for you often. Never expectation, it is hope my eyes have
      that your need for sun to keep your cold-blooded,
soft body
moving
within your
                hard shell

will coincide
      my desire: to see your body art
                      your neck
                                outstretched.
amplified exposure, reaching and spreading, thirsty to soak

I am thirsty to soak in you.
                    ~

I do not stand in wait for you to climb up the mud-dipped trunk.

The forest is not for me—   *life*   —but is.

I do not come here to wait for you. I catch you
                    catch me—
      in motion is how I always see you, but you
      are statue-still, soaking
      in every ray of natural,
      glitzy blessing, gawk, compliment, smile.

We both soak—or *all.* You, never alone, are nothing
if not social.

There is plenty of sun to go around on this day.
And I find you beautiful among your other selves.

~

I am in my intended role: at a   distance,   Alone Girl
      peaceful
-ly breathing steam
searching beauty to quench

                                 ~parched~

                WAIT

         you exit   [stage right]
splash right
back home out of my sight.

It's a whole other world down there. One the likes of me—not a
    diver—may never view. I will not see you there. I have
    held your beauty here with me now, and I am joyous, even
    at your exit.
(You can't leave unless you've been satisfied.)

THE COMMON CARP

David Hassler

Attention is the beginning of devotion.
—Mary Oliver

I remember how their large, slow-moving bodies
hung in the water under low birch branches
like burnished gold pendants, dull lanterns
shimmering in the dark current of the Cuyahoga.

As a child I meandered the riverbank, dragging a stick,
living those moments not in time but eternity.
The muddy river flowed through me,
seeped into my porous skin, the way water
soaked our basement floor after a heavy rain.
My sense of self was permeable.

Years later, still wandering, I arrived in Japan
and encountered the carp in a different
light, named in another tongue.
Bred for their colorful patterns,
treasured as living jewels, their name, koi,
means affection and love.
According to legend a carp swam upstream
and became a dragon.

Pollution tolerant and common in my Cuyahoga,
they are enshrined here in temple ponds,
flown as bright-colored windsocks atop poles,
swimming in currents of air.

Half-way around the world, in another language,

I return to my childhood river
and discover something about myself.
Standing on a small garden bridge,
staring down into the still, temple pond,
I see that what is common can be treasure,
what is slow is strong,
my muddy Cuyahoga still flowing.

Common Carp, *Cyprinus carpio*

YELLOW-DUSTED DREAMS:
THE MOTH HOUR

Cass Penegor

I had a dream the other night
That I was sitting with the Yellow-
Dusted Cream Moth. Together we sat
Near a stream eating blueberries, both of us silent

Only the sound of a warm May breeze
Moving through leaves.
I don't know how long
We sat there like that,
The Moth and I, near that stream,
Before we finally looked at one another. Tears
Filled my eyes, and the soft cream wings of
The Moth caught them as they fell. The Moth
Leaned towards me and embraced me, held me close.

The Moth whispered
In my ear its
Secrets—
We both knew I would not remember them when I awoke.
Swaddled in its wings, listening to its songs
Of mystery and
Wonder, I felt at peace—I felt
Understood,
Like we might not be so different.
I wish I could find you, Moth, outside
Of my dreams, outside of the dullness of December.

I would meet you in deciduous woods and together

We would lay in fallen leaves, and
Feel the warmth of the sunlight above us,
And I would tell you all of my secrets.
I'm compelled
To you, like you are
To a flame,
And each night I close my eyes, hoping my dreams

Take me back
To that stream where I will meet you again, Moth. The next
time, I promise, I will bring some willow Or maybe some
poplar with me, I know how you enjoy them.

Yellow-Dusted Cream Moth, *Cabera erythemaria*

BLUEGILL

Olivia Farina

I do not know how to swim but
that comes so naturally to you.
You move in ways I can only dream about
because you were built to dance in the water.
Even when you are frightened,
far away from your hidden water fortress,
you flit away from whoever seeks to harm you,
curved into a C,
dancing away.
I caught you once and
threw you back and
that is when I learned of your dance.
I couldn't stand to see myself hold
something so cosmically full of life.

You run like a machine:
Every muscle underneath scales and gills
is a work of art that keeps you alive.
Though your body is structured for movement and navigation,
you are still stuck.
When I see you in my dreams you are free and wild,
but in an instant you are taking oil into your terminal mouth,
drowning on sewage,
held trapped in plastic.
I try to remember you dancing
and not hooked at the end of a line.

Bluegill, *Lepomis macrochirus*

Warmouth, *Lepomis gulosus*

WARMOUTH SUNFISH

Camille Ferguson

Also called: molly, redeye, goggle-eye, red-eyed bream,
strawberry
       perch.
Mo-mouth, stumpknocker, limb-bream.

A mouthful.

You are mouthful. Some think
you're named for having *more mouth* than your relatives,
& that you've been mispronounced (warmouth/more
mouth/warmouth/more mouth) over time.
People say you're *all mouth,* which, as opposed to
being described as *all heart,* I can tell you
that's not a bad thing to be.
Often I daydream about discarding my heart
& letting everything it had been holding spill
out of my lips, which is to say I wish I was mouthier.

Others believe you're named for your stripes,
resembling warpaint used by Native Americans.
& others, still, offer an odd logic
on the origin of your name:
got a mouth so big you could have a war in it!

I think we relate too often in terms of violence.
So I call you something silly, like google-eye, like stumpknocker.
Sometimes we need something light.

You avoid the light, which is a funny thing for a sunfish
to do. You have teeth on your tongue, & rungs
along your throat like a ridged shell, or a mountainous cave.
If one were to only view you through your open mouth,
they would think you much larger than you are.

You eat almost anything—waterfleas,
aquatic sowbugs, crayfish, small crustaceans—
but you aren't often eaten. (People often describe
your taste as *muddy*. It is funny to expect a bottom
feeder to taste of something other than the bottom
of whatever water they feed in)
Some people do, catch & eat you.
They cook mudfish nuggets in hot grease.

It is lucky, however,
in this world, not to be devoured.

You are not intensely desired.

You are not in danger, yet.
You are, in fact, a *least concern*.
This is the best thing you can be.

(As a human, every time you learn about a creature,
especially one with goggle-eyes, gigantic mouths
& little stained glass mohawks, you must
google their conservation status, hold your breath & hope
for the words *least concern* to appear before you.)

You are in the water all around me, elusive,
hiding amongst vegetation, red-eyed,
golden-bellied, being mistaken for other fish

(rock-bass, green sunfish)
& called by names that don't fit
(*sun*fish, *war*mouth),
worrying only
about what to put into your very large mouth
    today & chew up with your tooth-speckled-tongue,
& deciding ultimately on what is nearest—delicious.

They say fish don't feel pain. I wish you could
open your enormous mouth & tell us.
I'm out here listening.

IN WHICH THE AMERICAN SYCAMORE AND I ARE FORMALLY INTRODUCED

Megan Lubey

It's summer and the American
Sycamore remembers—children bound by
plastic jump rope to her trunk,
the swift impact of pink handlebars
on bark. She knows, because she's been
whispered to, that love can be a dirty kitchen table,
pail and shovel at your feet.

You and I, American Sycamore, are the same,
both wrecked with autumn. Both exciting
ourselves bare. We are both so handsome!
We are both so hollow. Both gold and red
and brown. You in your fruit,
I, in my corduroy jacket. We both wish
childhood was closer once again.
Once again, you remember like the camera—
it is all lost on me.

In winter you are persistent and still standing—
this is where you and I differ. It is December and I
yearn & I yearn & you christmas yourself
with an easy harvest. You stand in vintage *Limited Too*
camouflage pants tinted blue as the snow-light washes
the indigo sky yellow. You're regal.
You're still glowing. Quiet, I think,
is a better word for cold.

American Sycamore! Look at that sky!
And you against it! The clouds melt
into rainbow sherbet. The ants tickle your skin.
Tenderness rides in with the breeze. I forgot the air
could carry sympathy. I remembered
when your dirt warmed. You knew.
You could always see further than me.
I sprout with the worms. We take shower after shower.
It's time to get clean again.

American Sycamore, *Platanus occidentalis*

AMERICAN FABLE: A TRUTH AS TOLD BY AMERICAN BEAVER

Katie Daley

Even though we circle the days
slick & nocturnal
and survey the underworld
with eyes closed
we inhabit ponderable Earth
alongside you
It's true, we've been endowed with
paddle-shaped tails
to slap like gunshots on river skin
webbed hind feet for superb swimming
& endlessly growing incisors
to fell Earth's trees & devise our shelters
But because our excellent pelts
keep their shapes & colors in the rain
we once appeared to colonists
as excellent hats
Our deaths became
for a time
all the rage
Despite our clever underwater entrances
& keen teeth
we brinked extinction
as did, in our wake, our neighbors:
trout, Ottawa, wetlands
the whole before
unperturbed
swath of Turtle Island

But like clouds, fashion doesn't tarry
only shapeshifts onward:
beaver to worm, pelt to silk
So listen
Now, beneath the scud
this swirl on river skin may speak
to you, may suggest
we burrow further than ever
into the deep, may warn
we still chew, slap, swill
& dream away our predators:
otter, cougar, mad hatters, humans
this story most of all

American Beaver, *Castor canadensis*

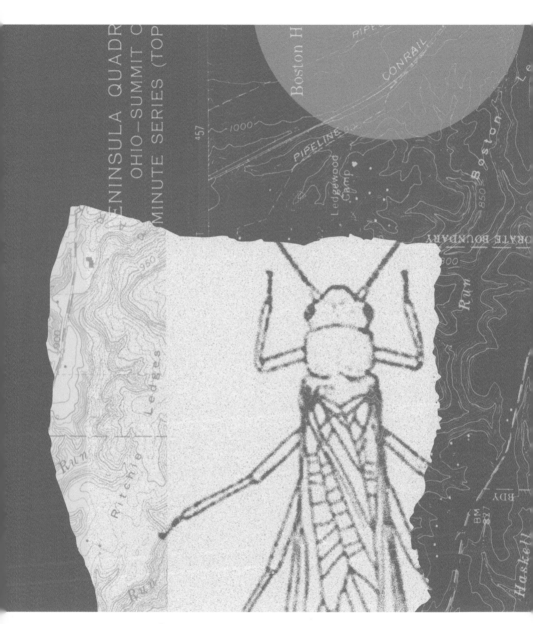

Common Stonefly, *Perlidae*

ODE TO THE PLECOPTERA

Karen Schubert

I sing you, common stonefly, and your 3500
families living everywhere except Antarctica,

coming to us straight from the Carboniferous
358.9 million years ago when atmospheric oxygen

reached its pinnacle and your ancestors
were big as flying cars. Now ribbons of oil.

You're the canaries in our clean streams, intolerant
of pollution where until recently, water

was pristine. I sing you, drab brown Plecoptera,
your Greek name meaning *braided wings,*

even if you prefer water over air, mandibles
feeding on sunken leaves and algae or

large compound eyes hunting arthropods.
After swimming as gilled nymph for years,

leap to land for one last molt, listen for a mate
drumming his belly for you. Then fly low over

the water to drop your thousand sticky eggs.

Yellow Bullhead, *Ameiurus natalis*

ODE TO A YELLOW BULLHEAD

Ted Lardner

What yellow, though!
Summer sunlight!
When it floods across
the end of the road,
under far rainclouds.
The downpour goes,
sluicing the grates
on the storm drains,
whooshing through
tunnels underground.
You live where rain
ends up at night, even
in daytime. Softly
on the bottom, down
in the dark, down
in quiet water. When
a child, I shined
a flashlight on you,
tangle of feelers—
barbels, whiskers—
what fell on you,
hanging in the air,
midnight, streamside,
a river we shared,
immense, patient,
folding away stars,
pocketing the ancient
light into its depth?
Red, alive in your eyes,

when that lost light
doubled back, fixing
on me, I shivered,
feeling seen, feeling
tasted. Did you talk?
Stridulate a secret
I needed, to survive
my life?
You go by
many names: yellow
cat, butter cat, creek
cat, yellow belly,
mud cat, hornpout;
Ameiurus natalis;
born of the family
Ictaluridae. In Texas
your cousins loved
the dark so much
they moved under-
ground, traded eyes,
the better to feel
as they navigated
the aquifers under
San Antonio by smell,
their way into the
mystery. One is
called Satan, the Widemouth
Blindcat. One is
called Phantom.
One, Toothless.
You have shovelheads,
Johnny cats and so,
so many madtoms,

their names flow over
a notebook page—
frecklebellies, piebalds,
Sciotos, Nooshos,
Ouchitas, saddled,
yellowfins, browns . . .

Like owls, active
at night, mostly;
social, you recognize
by smell, other yellow
bullheads; whiskers,
equally tongues, equally
hands. Fish that is cat,
your whole body,
a tongue: tastebuds
cover you all over;
you are inside-out;
you're a metaphor.
Your soul, your body,
the same density
as the water; you swim,
you breathe, water
that buoys you,
water you swim in—
swim bladder, pale as
boneset flowers, like an ear
inside your middle,
absorbing vibrations:
thud of mule hooves,
on the towpath,
a runner's stride,
traversing the stillness:

canal water: stillness
holds you: your fins,
namesake tail, patient,
fan the living current
over the eggs
in your nests. When
Creator bent this river
crooked—hard work—
sending it around,
corner after corner,
to loop back to
the source, to teach us
persistence, difficult
journeys, the work,
Creator got thirsty
and drank a little, sips
of the river, turning,
sip by sip, the water
in the river, sunlight
flavors, when yellow
seeps across fields
under coal seams
of thunderclouds.
Now from inside it,
on your tongue,
you hold the light
of the river, and wear
the sky, black on top,
yellow under, on your
body, tasting the river
so Creator can taste
the flow, the planet's
wide whirl: even the

suds, from Peninsula,
laundry run-off, matter,
fabric softeners,
floral fragrances and
sewerage, misting
the rapids, coating
the sills of the crumbled
lock chamber.

You school your babies.
Hundreds, a ladleful,
in a blue floating ball. Quivering,
rolling, spherical,
a compass, spelling
directions home, suspended
in the lull. Underbed
of reflections—faces,
forms, dogs, deer,
they sway, shimmer,
indigo globes; a shadow,
a whim, an ink drop;
consciousness,
descending into itself,
passing its silence
through us like a waved
wand, or a miniature
eclipse, a shadow
convergence above the
velvet silt. They drift,
a collective, a sense organ;
some awareness seems to
pass from them, out,
that calls us to

remember, to feel our
way deeper
into quiet; that calls
us to climb, down, down,
out of the noise, the terrifying
light, to let go of the
separateness, the acid
air of which, lodged
so deeply in our
throats, has burned so long,
a hook, a fire, we forget
is even there.

GREEN HERON
Paula J. Lambert

It's been hard for me to love Green Heron.
Homely, hidden, hardly moving at all, staring
into the depths, eyes made for that staring,

pointed permanently down, as if Sky never
mattered at all. How often we lift our eyes
to see her sisters soar: Great Blue, Egret,

those of the graceful glide, the long necks,
long legs, all while Green Heron hunches,
staring ever down, easy to overlook, so easy

not to see at all until she springs to action—
even then, we question what we've seen.
Praise the eater and the eaten, Joy Harjo says.

Praise beginnings; praise the end. Praise
our eyes now opened, praise understanding.
Praise the serpentine neck, suddenly retracted

and hidden again. Praise the fish swallowed.
I am the fish, writes Mary Oliver, *the fish
glitters in me; we are risen, tangled together,*

certain to fall back to the sea. Bless Green Heron
and her quietude. Bless beak become spear,
the javelin thrust. Bless homeliness, and bless

Green Heron, *Butorides virescens*

what it hides—bless all that it provides. Bless
the depths reflected, mirrored sky, the bird who
watches and who sees, bless the un-beautiful

creatures so quick to judge. Bless ignorance,
and patience, and forgiveness, and love. Bless
every new beginning. Bless everything that ends.

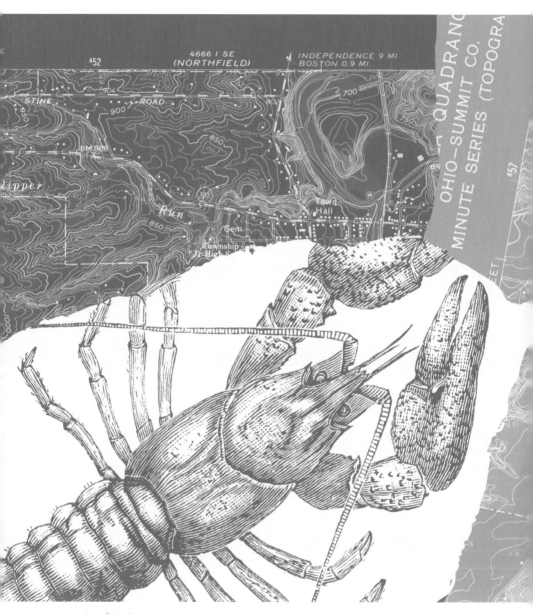

Crayfish, *Cambarus*

KNUCKLE

Conor Bracken

God is everywhere
but has his preferences.

Or she does. Or they.
Some pronoun that plunges

through the coarse
weave of language

like light through fog
as it fumbles, failing

again to laminate
the world.

                     God lurks
but not in majesty,

whatever the monks
in their stony redoubts say,

distilling the zing from high
meadows. Not in me, turning

rocks in the brook and
weighing the fate of the crayfish.

Maybe the crayfish? Shredding
the dead into silt, anxious

to shiver back into its niche
and sieve the current?

It curls in my hand
like a knuckle, or a hand

cupping flame. Some
absences burn. Some

can be held.

NOTES ON THE CONTRIBUTORS

Rebekah Ainsworth is a second-generation Clevelander, first-generation college graduate, and the descendant of many, many generations of mothers. Her essay collection, *Both And*, explores panic at the intersection of these and other roles. Rebekah teaches and tutors at Cuyahoga Community College.

Based in Columbus, Ohio, **Isaiah Yonah Back-Gaal** is a queer poet, climate justice organizer, and drag performer. They are currently an MFA candidate in creative writing at the Ohio State University and managing editor for *The Journal*. Their work has received support from *Seventh Wave Magazine* and the Greater Columbus Arts Council.

Lindsay Barba is a grant writer and poet. A lifelong northeast Ohioan, she grew up in Youngstown and studied creative writing at the University of Akron. Her work appears in *The Blue Windmill, SNAP, Poetry X Hunger, Poetry and Covid*, and here. She lives in Cuyahoga Falls and runs the trails of CVNP as often as she can.

Cathy Barber's poetry has been published in *Slant, SLAB*, the *Hopper, Stirring Journal*, and the anthologies *Rewilding: Poems for the Environment* and *Fire and Rain: Eco-poetry of California*. Her abecedarian chapbook is *Aardvarks, Bloodhounds, Catfish, Dingoes* (Dancing Girl Press, 2018) and her new, full-length book is *Once: A Golden Shovel Collection* (Kelsay Books, 2023). She is a graduate of the Vermont College of Fine Arts MFA program and makes her home in Cleveland Heights, Ohio.

Mary Biddinger's latest poetry collection is *Department of Elegy* (Black Lawrence Press, 2022). Her poems and flash fiction have recently appeared in *Always Crashing, DIAGRAM, Diode,* and *Pithead Chapel,* among others, and her work has been featured on *Poetry Daily* and *The Slowdown*. She edits the Akron Series in Poetry at the University of Akron Press and teaches creative writing at the University of Akron and the NEOMFA program.

Michelle Skupski Bissell is a lifelong resident of northeast Ohio and is thrilled to be included in this collection. She is serving her second term on the Strongsville Board of Education and is president of the Polaris Career Center Board of Education. She dedicates much of her time to wrangling the chaos of her four sons and three dogs, and she is a proud graduate of the NEOMFA (2009).

Marion Starling Boyer lives in Twinsburg, Ohio, and has published six poetry collections. Boyer's *Ice Hours* (2023) won the University of Michigan's Wheelbarrow prize and was named "New and Noteworthy" by *Poets & Writers*. Her chapbook, *What Word for This,* won Grayson Books's 2023 competition. Boyer conducts workshops for Lit Cleveland.

Conor Bracken is the author of *The Enemy of My Enemy Is Me* (Diode Editions, 2021), as well as the translator of Mohammed Khaïr-Eddine's *Scorpionic Sun* (CSU Poetry Center, 2019) and Jean D'Amérique's *No Way in the Skin without This Bloody Embrace* (Ugly Duckling Presse, 2022), a finalist for the 2023 PEN America's Award for Poetry in Translation. He teaches at the Cleveland Institute of Art.

Steve Brightman lives in Akron, Ohio, with his wife and their green parrot. He (Steve, not the parrot) firmly believes that there are only two seasons: winter and baseball.

Theresa Göttl Brightman's poems have appeared in many online and print publications, two chapbooks, and one full-length collection. She has received awards from the University of Akron and the City of Ventura, among others, and has been nominated for a Pushcart Prize, Rhysling Award, and Best of the Net. She lives in Akron with her husband and parrot, and she looks forward to watching the catbirds in their backyard every year.

Clara Britton is a recent graduate of Kent State University and is currently attending medical school. When she is not holed up at the library studying, she enjoys going on hikes and searching for lichen, which she believes is the paragon of romance. You can find more of her work in *Luna Negra* magazine.

Michael Buebe (he/him) is an artist from Galesburg Illinois. Author of *little spider cage (erotic velvet)* a micro-chapbook from Ghost City Press (2022). He has work out and forthcoming in *Common Ground Review*'s Annual Poem Contest (honorable mention 2021), *Pinhole Poetry, TIMBER, Lover's Eye Press,* and *Kissing Dynamite.*

KJ Cerankowski is the author of the critical lyric memoir *Suture: Trauma and Trans Becoming.* His poetry and prose have also been published in *DIAGRAM, Pleiades, Sinister Wisdom,* and *Gordon Square Review,* among others. He teaches at Oberlin College.

Kathleen Cerveny is a potter, a poet, and a lifelong arts advocate. She directed the Cleveland Foundation's arts grantmaking until her retirement in 2014, completing her MFA in creative writing the same year. Her poems have been published in numerous journals, and a chapbook, *Coming to Terms,* was published by Night Ballet Press in 2016.

Sylvia Clark (she/they) is a poet based in Kent, Ohio. She graduated with a BA in English from Kent State University with a minor in creative writing. They do what they can to earn their own awareness.

Jonathan Conley is a writer and musician from Cleveland. He is the author of the chapbook *House Hunters International: Sonnets* (Seven Kitchens Press, 2023) and founder of *Yum! Lit.*

Katie Daley has received three Individual Excellence Awards from the Ohio Arts Council and has performed her work across North America on street corners and riverbanks and in ballrooms and saloons. Her chapbook of poems, *Any Closer to Home,* came out in October 2023 from Finishing Line Press.

Dan Dorman's most recent writing can be found at the Cuyahoga Public Library and *Bangalore Review,* with visual poems at Word for/Word and others. He graduated from the NEOMFA and teaches creative writing and composition on a wandering basis.

Olivia Farina (she/her) is a writer from Cleveland, Ohio. Her writing focuses on the body, generational trauma, and the grand spectrum of human emotions. Her work can be found in *Luna Negra* magazine, *Sink Hollow* magazine, and in a forthcoming *Alternative Field* anthology.

Camille Ferguson is a poet from Ohio who is currently doing seasonal work across the country, living and working in National Parks. They believe the only constant is change and strive to be comfortable being uncomfortable; therefore, they don't stay in any one place for too long. Camille's work has been published in *Flypaper Lit, Door Is a Jar,* and *Passages North,* among others.

Deborah Fleming's nonfiction collection *Resurrection of the Wild: Meditations on Ohio's Natural Landscape* (2019) won the PEN America's Diamonstein-Spielvogel Award for the Art of the Essay for 2020. She is the author of three collections of poems, *Morning, Winter Solstice* (2012), *Into a New Country* (2016), and *Earthrise* (2021); chapbooks *Migrations* (2005) and *Source of the River* (2018); and two novels, *Without Leave* (2014), winner of the Asheville Award, and *Reunion* (forthcoming). She served for many years as director and editor of the Ashland Poetry Press.

Dr. R. Ray Gehani has been a multidisciplinary lifelong learner, a university educator, and a creative innovator integrating his techno-scientific mind with his artistic heart. Dr. Gehani has cocurated *Turning Leaves: An Anthology of Prose and Poetry* (poetry by northeastern Ohio writers) and has chaired Akron Creative Writers' Roundtable for 12 years. He has published nine nonfiction books and six poetry chapbooks, hoping that his best book is still ahead soon.

Carrie George is a poet and teacher living in Akron, Ohio. She received her MFA from Kent State University and the NEOMFA program. She is the manager at Elizabeth's Bookshop & Writing Centre. Her work has appeared in *Hayden's Ferry Review,* the *Florida Review, Cosmonauts Avenue,* the *Indianapolis Review,* and elsewhere.

Andrew Gilkey is a writer from Cincinnati, Ohio. You can find more of his work in *Mock Turtle Zine* and the *Carroll Review.*

Stephanie Ginese is an author and stand-up comedian from South Lorain, Ohio. Her debut collection of poetry, *Unto Dogs,* was released in July 2022 by Grieveland. Currently, she lives in Cleveland with her two children.

Cameron Gorman is a writer, artist, and journalist living in Ohio. Cameron's work has been published in outlets such as the *Rumpus, Slate,* and *Juked.*

Leah Graham is an environmental educator and artist. She earned an MS in environmental studies from Ohio University, researching nesting ecology of diamondback terrapins in the Chesapeake; a BS in environmental biology from Mount Union College; and a graduate certificate in scientific illustration from the University of Washington. She has served Kent State University's Office of Sustainability since 2013, currently as the sustainability coordinator. With her husband and children, she lives on an old street with tall oaks near the Cuyahoga River.

Jeff Gundy's 13 books include *Wind Farm: Landscape with Stories and Towers*, *Without a Plea*, and *Abandoned Homeland*. A former Fulbright lecturer in Salzburg, Austria, his work appears in *Georgia Review*, the *Sun*, *Kenyon Review*, *Forklift, Ohio*, *Christian Century*, *Image*, *Cincinnati Review*, and *Terrain.org*. He was named Ohio Poet of the Year for *Somewhere Near Defiance* and received a grant from the Seattle Foundation to serve as 2023–24 Writer in (Non)Residence at Bluffton University.

Kari Gunter-Seymour is the Poet Laureate of Ohio. She is the founder/executive director of the Women of Appalachia Project and editor of its anthology series *Women Speak*. Her work has been featured in *Verse Daily*, *World Literature Today*, the *New York Times*, and *Poem-a-Day*.

Jason Harris is a Black American writer, editor, and teaching artist. He currently serves as editor in chief for *Gordon Square Review*. He has received fellowships from the Watering Hole and Twelve Literary Arts.

Residing in Cleveland, Ohio, **Quartez Harris** is the Ohio Poetry Association's 2021 Poet of the Year and the author of *We Made It to School Alive*, a full-length collection of poems. Harris is represented by McKinnon Literary Agency. His works in progress include two picture books and a middle-grade novel.

David Hassler is the author or editor of 10 books of poetry and nonfiction. He is the Bob and Walt Wick Executive Director of the Wick Poetry Center at Kent State University. His awards include Ohio Poet of the Year, the Ohioana Book Award, the Carter G. Woodson Honor Book Award, and two Ohio Arts Council Individual Excellence Awards. Additionally, he has coauthored articles on poetry, technology, and healing in such journals as the *Journal of Palliative Medicine* and the *Online Journal of Issues in Nursing*.

Born and raised as a proud Cleveland native, **Isaiah Hunt** focuses on near-future stories of his community, commercialism, the entertainment industry, and trans-humanist capitalism. Currently he teaches fiction writing at John Carroll University as a Hopkins Fellow. You can find his work at *Luna Negra, On the Run, Black Moon Magazine, What If Tomorrow, Catchwater Magazine,* and elsewhere.

Andrea Imdacha is a writer and poet of Sri Lankan and Hungarian heritage who hails from Savannah, Georgia. Her poetry and short fiction have appeared in several publications, including *North American Review, Literary Mama,* and *Mash Stories.* Her work has been shortlisted for the Kurt Vonnegut Prize in Speculative Literature and the James Kirkwood Prize in Fiction. Andrea lives in Cleveland, Ohio, with her husband and son.

Kimberlee Medicine Horn is an Indigenous poet from the Ihanktonwan Nation. Her work has appeared in the *Yellow Medicine Review,* the *South Dakota Quarterly, Common Threads,* and elsewhere. Jackson writes about nature from her Indigenous perspective and also explores the intersection between Indigeneity and Christianity.

Jessica Jewell is the author of four collections of poetry, *Tender, Tender* (Headmistress Press; winner of the Charlotte Mew Prize), *Dust Runner* (Finishing Line Press), *Sisi and the Girl from Town* (Finishing Line Press), and *Slap Leather* (dancing girl press). She is the coeditor of the bilingual collection *I Hear the World Sing* (Kent State University Press). Jewell is the senior academic program director for the Wick Poetry Center at Kent State University, where she also earned her PhD and MFA.

Jessica Jones (MA, University Montana) is full-time faculty at Kent State University at Stark, where she teaches poetry, Native American literature, and composition courses that focus on social justice. She also regularly teaches on two reservations in Indian Country. Her book, *Bitterroot* (2018), can be found at Finishing Line Press.

Monica Kaiser is a published poet, tree hugger, nature lover, rabbit rescuer, and author of a collection of poems, *Still Sifting* (Mellen Poetry Press). She holds an MFA in creative writing from Kent State University and lives with her partner, their son, two rabbits, and her dad.

Bob King is a professor of English at Kent State University at Stark. His poetry collection *And & And* is forthcoming from Finishing Line Press in August 2024, and another collection, *And/Or*, is forthcoming in September 2025. He lives in Fairview Park, Ohio, with his wife and daughters.

Virginia Konchan is the author of four poetry collections, *Bel Canto* (Carnegie Mellon University Press, 2022), *Hallelujah Time* (Véhicule Press, 2021), *Any God Will Do* (Carnegie Mellon, 2020), and *The End of Spectacle* (Carnegie Mellon, 2018); the author of a collection of short stories, *Anatomical Gift;* and the coeditor of the craft anthology *Marbles on the Floor: How to Assemble a Book of Poems* (University of Akron Press, 2023). Her poems have appeared in the *New Yorker*, the *New Republic*, the *Atlantic*, *American Poetry Review*, the *Believer*, and the *Academy of American Poets*.

Sujata Lakhe grew up in Bhilai, India. She immigrated to Cleveland in her early twenties. Her writing interests include poems, essays, memoirs, and short stories. She has published in *Neighborhood Voices*, the *Blue Windmill*, *Scene*, the *Lotus*, *Literary Cleveland Blogs*, and peer-reviewed scientific journals, and she has performed her work at the Story Club, Photocentric, and Valley Art Center and Heights Arts. She presently serves as the president on the Board of Literary Cleveland.

Paula J. Lambert has published several collections of poetry, including *The Ghost of Every Feathered Thing* (FutureCycle, 2022) and *How to See the World* (Bottom Dog, 2020). Awarded PEN America's l'Engle-Rahman Prize for Mentorship, Lambert's poetry and prose has been supported by the Ohio Arts Council, the Greater Columbus Arts Council, and the Virginia Center for Creative Arts. She lives in Columbus with her husband Michael Perkins, a philosopher and technologist.

Ted Lardner is an avid native plants gardener and yoga teacher. His writing has recently appeared in *One*, *About Place Journal*, and *Missouri Review*'s poem of the week. *Tornado*, a chapbook, is available from the Kent State University Press.

Cora McCann Liderbach lives on the shores of Lake Erie in Lakewood, Ohio. Her poetry has appeared in *Last Stanza Poetry Journal*, the *RavensPerch*, *Poem for Cleveland Anthology*, *Crab Creek Review*, *Ohio Bards Anthology*, *LunaNegra Online*, *Ariel's Dream Journal*, *Imposter Literary Journal*, and *Broadkill Review*. She was also a finalist in *Gordon Square Review*'s 2022 Contest for Ohio Writers.

Eros Livieratos (he/they) is a Greek-Belizean writer and artist whose work focuses on the intersection of identity, aesthetics, and capital in the Anthropocene. Eros has published poetry, fiction, nonfiction, comics, photography, and film score work. They can usually be found making harsh noise and screaming in your local basement.

Michael Loderstedt's first book of poems, *Why We Fished*, was published by Redhawk Publications in April 2023. The title poem received honorable mention in the 2023 Jaki Shelton Green Performance Poetry Competition. Loderstedt's recent writings have been featured in *Muleskinner Journal*, the *NC Literary Review*, *Bangalore Review, Poem for Cleveland*, and *Musepaper*. He received a 2020 Ohio Arts Council Fellowship in Literature for his memoir manuscript *The Yellowhammer's Cross*. He is professor emeritus of Kent State University's School of Art where he taught printmaking and photography. He currently lives in Cleveland, Ohio, near the shore of Lake Erie with his wife Lori and son Ethan.

Megan Lubey is a visual artist and writer currently located in Cleveland, Ohio. They graduated from the Cleveland Institute of Art in 2022 with a degree in painting. Lubey is also the author of a chapbook titled *About Cutting Limes and the Moon Being in Half.*

Diana Lueptow is the author of *Little Nest* (Wick chapbook, Kent State University Press, 2015) and poems in many journals and the recipient of three Individual Excellence Awards from the Ohio Arts Council. She lives a few miles from CVNP and is a longtime supporter of its beauties.

Chad W. Lutz is a speedy, bipolar writer born in Akron, Ohio, in 1986, and raised in the neighboring suburb of Stow. They graduated from Mills College in Oakland, California, with their MFA in creative writing in 2018. Their first book, *For the Time Being* (2020), is currently available through J.New Books. Other recent works appear in *Haunted Waters Press, Drunk Monkeys, Half and One*, and *Hunger Mountain Review*.

Charles Malone works with writers in the community around Kent, Ohio. His poetry collections include *After an Eclipse of Moths* (Moonstone), *Working Hypothesis*

(Finishing Line Press), and *Questions About Circulation* (Driftwood Press). He edited the collection *A Poetic Inventory of Rocky Mountain National Park* with Wolverine Farm Publishing. Charles now works at the Wick Poetry Center at Kent State.

Judith Mansour has worked as editor and associate publisher for *Northern Ohio Live Magazine*, contributing editor for *angle* magazine, and publisher for Fresh Water Cleveland. During her tenure as executive director of the LIT: Cleveland's Literary Center, she and art director Tim Lachina created *MUSE*, a magazine that focused on the interplay of words and images. In 2022 Mansour published her first full-length collection of prose and poetry, *Kan Zaman*, with Crisis Chronicles Press. Her life is ruled by love of her family, words, food, and a pack of unruly cats.

Delilah McCrea is a trans-anarchist poet. She loves the NBA and knows the lyrics to every Saintseneca song. Her work can be found in *Vagabond City, Gordon Square Review, Petrichor, Night Coffee Lit,* and *Hobart After Dark.*

Ray McNiece has authored 11 books of poems, monologues, and poetry/music CDs. He has received a Creative Work Force Fellowship, a CPAC grant, and residencies at Cuyahoga Valley National Park and the Jack Kerouac House. He received the Cleveland Arts Prize Lifetime Achievement Award in 2021 and was Awarded a $50,000 Poet Laureate Grant from the American Academy of Poetry for his Poem for Cleveland Project in 2022, from which the anthology *Poem for Cleveland* was created.

Anastasios Mihalopoulos is a Greek/Italian American from Boardman, Ohio. He received his MFA in poetry from the NEOMFA program and his BS in both chemistry and English from Allegheny College. His work has appeared in *Blue Earth Review, West Trade Review, Ergon,* the *Decadent Review,* and elsewhere. He is currently pursuing a PhD in creative writing and literature at the University of New Brunswick.

Dr. Susann Moeller, vice president of OPA, is an award-winning bilingual poet and editor of the eco-poetry anthologies *Open Earth I, II,* and *III.* She believes in the inseparable nature of art and the environment as poetry enriches every type of experience and vice versa.

Kortney Morrow is a poet creating from her studio in Cleveland, Ohio. Her work has received support from *68t005*, the *Academy of American Poets*, *Obsidian*, *Prairie Schooner*, the Studio Museum in Harlem, *Tin House*, and *Transition Magazine*. She is the winner of the 2023 Ohioana Library Association Walter Rumsey Marvin Grant and has her MFA in creative writing from the Ohio State University.

Risha Nicole is a poet, author, and teaching artist from Sandusky, Ohio. She has a BA in English from Kent State University. She is the author of her full-length poetry book, *Without a Sound*, and her first chapbook *As Long As I Live You Are with Me*.

Courtney Noster is a daughter of the Great Lakes that spends her days wandering trails and falling in love with nature. She is a poet, musician, and counselor who is passionate about connecting with other people and building earth-centered communities.

Caryl Pagel's most recent books are *Free Clean Fill Dirt* (poetry, University of Akron Press) and *Out Of Nowhere Into Nothing* (essays, FC2). She is a cofounder of and editor at Rescue Press and directs the CSU Poetry Center. Pagel teaches at Cleveland State University and in the NEOMFA program.

Cass Penegor is an artist currently based in Lakewood, Ohio. They received their BFA from the Cleveland Institute of Art and their MFA from Cranbrook Academy of Art. Their work has been featured in various online exhibitions, and they have shown work in galleries across northeast Ohio and Michigan. Cass loves theater, coffee, and mini-muffins, and their favorite color is yellow (no matter what anyone else says).

Alyssa Perry's writing appears in *Annulet, The Canary, Fence,* and elsewhere. A book, *Oily Doily,* is forthcoming from Bench Editions in fall 2024. Perry is an editor at Rescue Press and *Cleveland Review of Books*. Perry teaches at the Cleveland Institute of Art.

Hilary Plum is a writer, editor, and teacher living in Cleveland Heights. Her recent work includes *Excisions*, a volume of poetry; *Hole Studies*, an essay collection;

and the novel *Strawberry Fields,* which won the Fence Modern Prize in Prose. She teaches at Cleveland State and in the NEOMFA program, and she serves as associate director of the CSU Poetry Center.

Geoffrey Polk started the street poetry team Poetry Free Cleveland, teaches English at Lorain County Community College, and plays jazz saxophone and clarinet. He attended Berklee College of Music and has an MA in English from Cleveland State University, where he was editor of *Whiskey Island.*

Kira Preneta (she, her/they, them) was born just west of Lake Superior and feels most at home near big water. Their writing is often referred to as a gift, a gift they are happy to give and receive. As a mother to four children, claiming time for their voice to meet the page is a lesson in inhabiting liminal. Kira currently resides in the suburban/rural wilds of the North American Rust Belt, just south of Lake Erie.

The recipient of four Ohio Arts Council Individual Excellence Awards for both poetry and nonfiction, **Mary Quade** is the author of the poetry collections *Guide to Native Beasts* (CSU Poetry Center) and *Local Extinctions* (Gold Wake). Her essay collection *Zoo World: Essays* (Ohio State University Press/Mad Creek Books) won the 2022 Journal Non/Fiction Prize. She teaches at Hiram College.

Benjamin Anthony Rhodes is a queer and trans poet living in northeast Ohio. He's earned an MFA in creative writing from Kent State University and a BA in English from the University of Louisiana at Monroe. Benjamin carries on his mother's legacy by teaching reading and writing to students of all ages. His work can be found in *Cleveland Review of Books, Cowboy Jamboree, Surging Tide, Let Me Say This: A Dolly Parton Poetry Anthology,* and elsewhere.

Barbara Sabol's sixth collection, *WATERMARK,* is forthcoming from Alternating Currents Press. She is the associate editor of *Sheila-Na-Gig* online. Barbara conducts poetry workshops through Literary Cleveland. She lives in Akron, Ohio, with her husband and wonder dogs.

Shei Sanchez writes from the woods and meadows of her farm in Appalachian Ohio. Her work can be found in many journals, anthologies, and projects, including *Still: The Journal, Women of Appalachia Project's Women Speak, Sheila-Na-Gig, Les Délices Music Meditations,* and *One* by Jacar Press. Shei has had the pleasure of collaborating with many northeastern Ohio writers over the past few years and is forever working on her first collection of poems.

Zach Savich is the author of nine books of poetry and nonfiction, including *Momently* (Black Ocean, 2024). He teaches at the Cleveland Institute of Art.

Karen Schubert is the author of *The Compost Reader* (Accents Publishing) and five chapbooks, including *I Left My Wings on a Chair* (Kent State University Press), winner of a Wick Poetry Center Chapbook Prize. Her poetry was recently performed at the Cleveland Humanities Festival and published in the *Poem for Cleveland* project, Edith Chase Symposium anthology *Songs for Wild Ohio,* the *Pinch,* and Ohio Poetry Association's *Common Threads.* Her awards include an Ohio Arts Council Individual Excellence Award and residencies at the Vermont Studio Center and Headlands Center for the Arts. She is the founding director of Lit Youngstown.

Amanda Schuster was born and raised in the Cleveland area and grew up exploring CVNP. Her background is in formal education and language arts, and she has a MA in science education for adult fitness and exercise physiology. She has been with the Conservancy since 2015 and is currently the director of the Cuyahoga Valley Environmental Education Center. Amanda was part of a national cohort that coauthored a best practice guide for social-emotional learning in residential environmental education and was part of a regional cohort that focused on centering racial equity in environmental education. When she's not working in Cuyahoga, she's probably in another park somewhere, most likely looking at birds. When at home, Amanda enjoys playing music, watching movies, or spending time with family.

Haylee Schwenk is a poet and editor who is passionate about the many communities that hold her up and save her life, over and over. She grew up a half acre from where a country stream empties into a winding creek and has lived a mile or less from Lake Erie for over 30 years now. She loves to visit any kind of water: lake, stream, river, creek, pond, marsh, or abandoned canal. Her work has been published in *Great Lakes Review, Q/A, Sheila-Na-Gig, Panoply,* and *Pudding Magazine.*

Tovli Simiryan ("Linnie") is an award-winning writer currently living in northeast Ohio with her husband, Yosif. She has published two books of poetry, *The Breaking of the Glass* and *Fixing the Broken Glass,* and a collection of short fiction, *Ruach of the Elders—Spiritual Teachings of the Silent.*

Zachary Thomas has served as the inaugural Anisfield-Wolf Book Awards Fellow since 2018. He is also the executive director of Writers in Residence, which he cofounded as an undergraduate at John Carroll University. He earned his BA in creative and professional writing and Literature and his MA in nonprofit administration. After more than a decade, he finally calls Cleveland home. When he's not empowering youth in detention to write, he's encouraging himself to do the same. His work appears in the *John Carroll Review* and the *Blue Route.*

Bronlynn Thurman is a creative and nonprofit professional in the Akron area. Her work is often inspired by the natural world and its ability to induce wonder and awe. Thurman holds a BS in advertising and an MS in information architecture and knowledge management from Kent State University.

Born in Odesa, Ukraine, **Marina Vladova** (MPH, MEd, CHW) finds herself thinking and writing about gooseberries, resettlement, and migratory loss. In nature, she sees belongingness. Marina is a writer, educator, and narrative medicine facilitator. Her work connects patients, practitioners, and communities. Marina enjoys collaborating interprofessionally and is currently working toward her CPA in narrative medicine through Columbia University.

Laura Grace Weldon lives in a township too tiny for traffic lights where she works as a book editor, teaches writing workshops, and maxes out her library card each week. Laura served as Ohio's 2019 Poet of the Year and is the author of four books.

Catherine Wing is the author of two collections of poetry, *Enter Invisible* and *Gin & Bleach.* Her poems have been published in such journals as *Poetry,* the *Nation,* and *Tin House.* She teaches at Kent State University and with the NEOMFA, the nation's only consortial program in creative writing.

Rebecca Wohlever is a forest-dwelling, storytelling songstress who dreams of one day becoming a mermaid. When she isn't leading forest school programs, teaching yoga, or performing music locally, you can find her goofing around with her children or playing frisbee with the best dog in the world. Her music can be found anywhere you can find music, and her poetry can be found in notebooks scattered throughout her home.

Tishon Woolcock is a poet and a maker of things. He was a Poets House Emerging Poets Fellow (2014). He designs museums for a living and writes poetry for life.

Caitie Young (they/them) is a poet and writer from Kent, Ohio. Their work has appeared or is forthcoming in the *Sonora Review,* the *Minnesota Review, Scapegoat, Passengers Journal, Vallum, Foothill,* and elsewhere. They were the first-place recipient of the 2022 Foothill Editors Prize for best graduate student poetry, and they are a Pushcart nominee. Caitie is currently studying creative writing in the NEOMFA program and teaching workshops as the Wick Poetry Center Graduate Teaching Artist.